Life Processes

How a Living Thing Stays Alive

DEVELOPED IN COOPERATION
WITH

ST. LOUIS SCIENCE CENTER
ST. LOUIS, MISSOURI

Copyright © 1997, 1995 by Scholastic Inc. All rights reserved.
Published by Scholastic Inc.
Printed in the U.S.A.

ISBN 0-590-95514-4

2 3 4 5 6 7 8 9 10   09   03 02 01 00 99 98 97 96

LIVING THINGS ARE DIVERSE, INTERDEPENDENT, AND EVOLVING.

Life Processes

All organisms perform basic life processes.

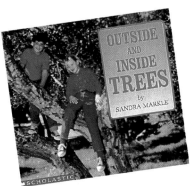

A Recipe for Staying Alive

A hummingbird beats its wings 70 times a second as it flies from flower to flower hunting for food. Some ants can pick up pieces of food that are 50 times heavier than their own bodies. A male seahorse hatches its mate's eggs in a pouch on its belly. The things organisms do to stay alive are truly incredible.

And what about you? Your body does some amazing things to keep you alive. All living things have to do certain things — life processes — to stay alive.

What do you know about life processes?

Because you're a living organism, you already know some of the things organisms have to do to stay alive. Work with your class to make a list of what you already know.

What do you want to know?

Make a second list with your class. This time, list questions you have about the ways living things work. For example, what are all the little dots in the picture?

How will you find out?

You'll work in teams to discover many of the answers to your questions. You'll share what you learn with other teams in your class. You'll also find out what other scientists have discovered about life processes.

The table of contents on pages 2 and 3 shows the problems you're going to solve in this unit. In each exploration lesson, you and your team will use scientific methods to solve the problem:

• You'll make a *hypothesis* — a prediction — about possible answers to the problem.

• You'll do a *hands-on exploration* — maybe two — that will help you test your hypothesis. Much of your hands-on work in this unit will be with plants. You'll grow them, observe how they perform their life processes, and compare them with other living things — including yourself.

• You'll *record data* you collect.

• You'll *draw conclusions* from your data.

• You'll *compare* your conclusions to those of other teams in your class.

• You'll *apply* your conclusions to your own life.

What Are Living Things Made Of?

How would you describe a living thing? You know that you're one, and your teacher's one, too. So are bees and trees. You know you're different from a bee in many ways, but in some ways you and a bee are alike. And both you and a bee have things in common with all other living things. Comparing different kinds of living things with each other and with nonliving things is a good way to start understanding exactly what a living thing is.

Exploration
Observe your neighbors.

You need:
Hand lens
Pencil
Paper

❶ Look around your classroom. How many different kinds of living things can you find? Start a list. ✏

❷ Go outside. See how many different kinds of living things you can find on the school grounds. Add these living things to your list. ✏

❸ Back in the classroom, compare your list with the lists of your classmates. Then make one list for the entire class. Include each kind of living thing the class observed.

Interpret your results.

• How did you decide that the things you observed were living things and not nonliving things?

• What kinds of structures are similar in different living things you found?

• Was it hard to decide whether some things were living or nonliving? Explain.

HOW A CAT IS ORGANIZED

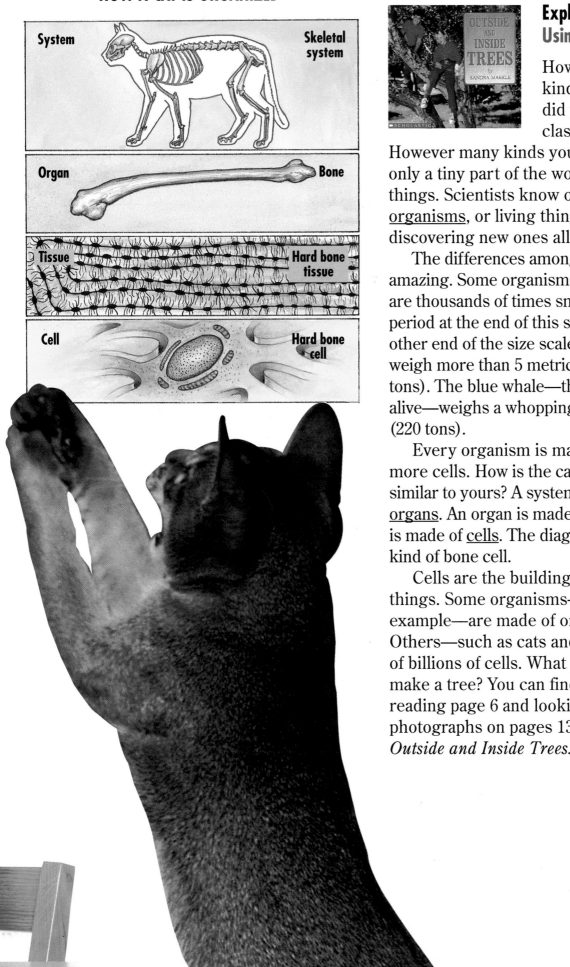

System — Skeletal system

Organ — Bone

Tissue — Hard bone tissue

Cell — Hard bone cell

**Exploration Connection:
Using reference books**

How many different kinds of living things did you and your classmates observe? However many kinds you found, they're only a tiny part of the world of living things. Scientists know of nearly 2 million <u>organisms</u>, or living things, and they're discovering new ones all the time.

The differences among organisms are amazing. Some organisms called bacteria are thousands of times smaller than the period at the end of this sentence. At the other end of the size scale, elephants can weigh more than 5 metric tons (about 6 tons). The blue whale—the largest animal alive—weighs a whopping 200 metric tons (220 tons).

Every organism is made up of one or more cells. How is the cat's skeletal <u>system</u> similar to yours? A system is made up of <u>organs</u>. An organ is made of <u>tissues</u>. A tissue is made of <u>cells</u>. The diagram shows one kind of bone cell.

Cells are the building blocks of living things. Some organisms—bacteria, for example—are made of only one cell. Others—such as cats and trees—are made of billions of cells. What kinds of cells make a tree? You can find some answers by reading page 6 and looking at the photographs on pages 13, 14, and 16 of *Outside and Inside Trees.*

Closer to Home:
Your building blocks

You're an organism. That means you're made up of cells—billions of cells and lots of different kinds of cells. For example, the outer part of your body is made of skin cells that fit together like the tiles in a floor. These cells form a protective covering for your body. Skin is amazing stuff: It's stain-resistant, stretchable, and waterproof. That's why you don't soak up water like a sponge when you go swimming. That's also why you aren't all dried up like a prune—your waterproof skin keeps moisture inside your body.

Other kinds of cells make up your muscles. Muscle cells have a design that allows your body to move. You know about the muscles that move your arms and legs. Other muscles move your ribs, allowing you to breathe. The moving muscles of your heart cause it to beat and move blood through your body. Muscles in your stomach toss and turn food, helping you to digest it. What other muscles do you know about?

You have other kinds of cells, too. Each kind of cell in your body is part of a tissue that's part of an organ that's part of a system—that's part of you. Look at the diagram to see one kind of cell that's part of the system that lets you breathe. In what organ could you find tissue made of these cells? What other organs join with this one to form the respiratory system?

• What is one way you and all other living things are alike?

• All the jobs that different cells, tissues, organs, and systems do for your body have to be done by just the single cell of a one-celled organism. What do you think are the advantages for your body of having many different kinds of cells to carry out different jobs?

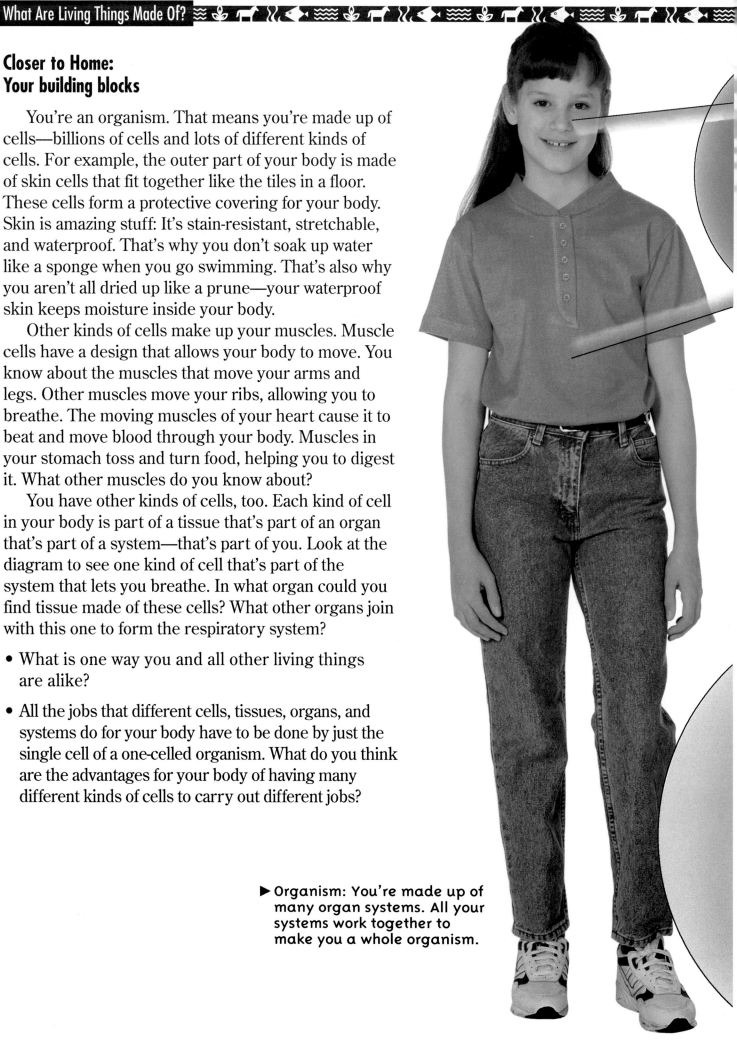

▶ Organism: You're made up of many organ systems. All your systems work together to make you a whole organism.

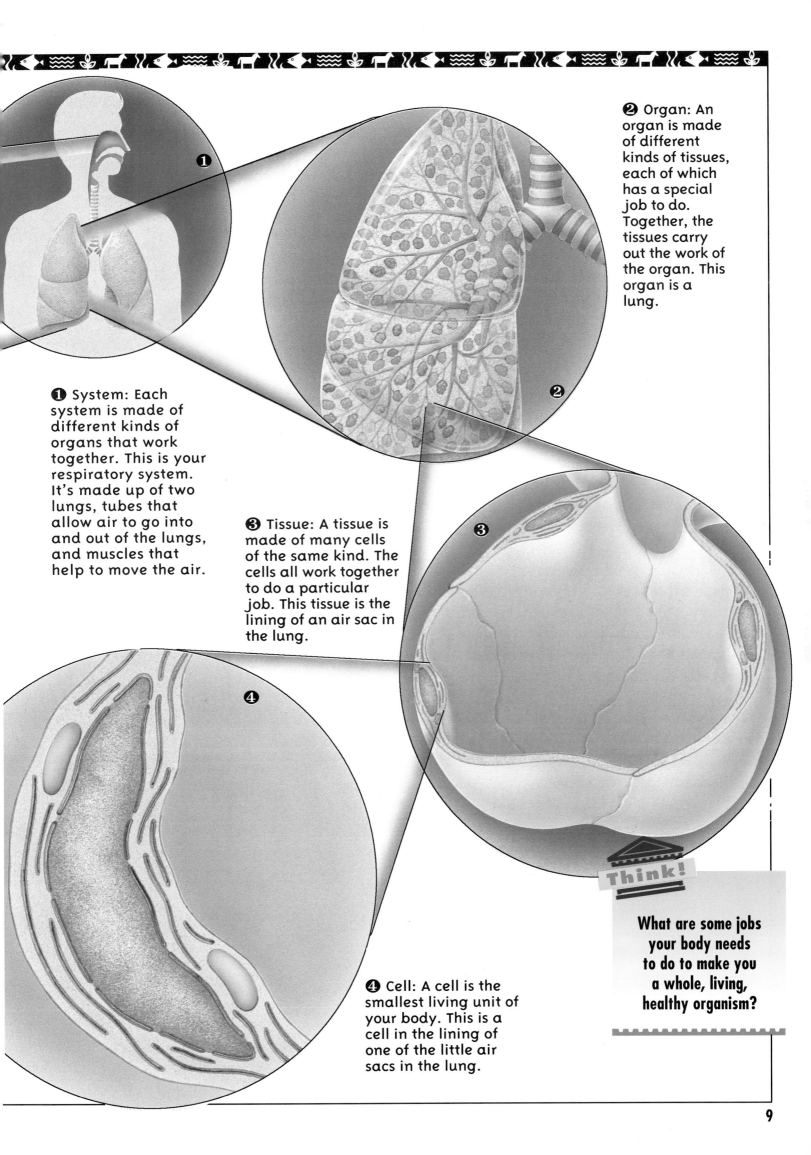

❶ System: Each system is made of different kinds of organs that work together. This is your respiratory system. It's made up of two lungs, tubes that allow air to go into and out of the lungs, and muscles that help to move the air.

❷ Organ: An organ is made of different kinds of tissues, each of which has a special job to do. Together, the tissues carry out the work of the organ. This organ is a lung.

❸ Tissue: A tissue is made of many cells of the same kind. The cells all work together to do a particular job. This tissue is the lining of an air sac in the lung.

❹ Cell: A cell is the smallest living unit of your body. This is a cell in the lining of one of the little air sacs in the lung.

Think!

What are some jobs your body needs to do to make you a whole, living, healthy organism?

What Do Living Things Do to Stay Alive?

When you find an organism you've never seen before, compare it with the living things you've observed. One thing you'll know for sure—it's made up of cells. If the organism is big enough for you to be able to see it, its cells are parts of tissues, organs, and systems. All these body parts do things that keep the organism alive. That's another thing all organisms have in common—they have to do certain things to stay alive. What do you do to stay alive?

A Day in Some Lives

Suppose you could observe one day in the life of several different organisms: a great white shark, a bald eagle, a butterfly, a Venus's-flytrap, and a bamboo plant. The longer you watched each of them, the more you'd see that they are all alike in some ways.

A great white shark swims constantly. It has to keep moving so that water passes over its gills. Gills are organs that the shark uses to take oxygen in from the water. The shark's keen senses help the shark in its search for food.

A bald eagle soars through the sky and swoops down to catch its prey. The eagle's speed and sharp eyesight make it a good hunter. The eagle carries the food back to the nest, where its mate is sitting on the eggs, keeping them warm.

A hard shell-like object suddenly starts to crack open. Within minutes, a butterfly pulls itself free of the shell. Before the butterfly was in the shell, it was a caterpillar, eating green plants. Now it's going to suck nectar from flowers.

A fly is buzzing around a Venus's-flytrap. Oops! The fly lands on part of the plant's leaf. Tiny hairs feel the fly landing, and the leaf snaps shut. The fly is trapped and becomes food for the plant.

A bamboo plant is a fast grower. During one day, a bamboo plant can grow 90 cm (3 ft)! A bamboo plant may eventually grow to be 30 m (98 ft) tall. The bamboo plant gets light through its leaves and water through its roots.

Think about these descriptions. What do these organisms have in common? Work with your classmates to make a checklist of things you think a living thing *must* do to stay alive. These activities are called life processes.

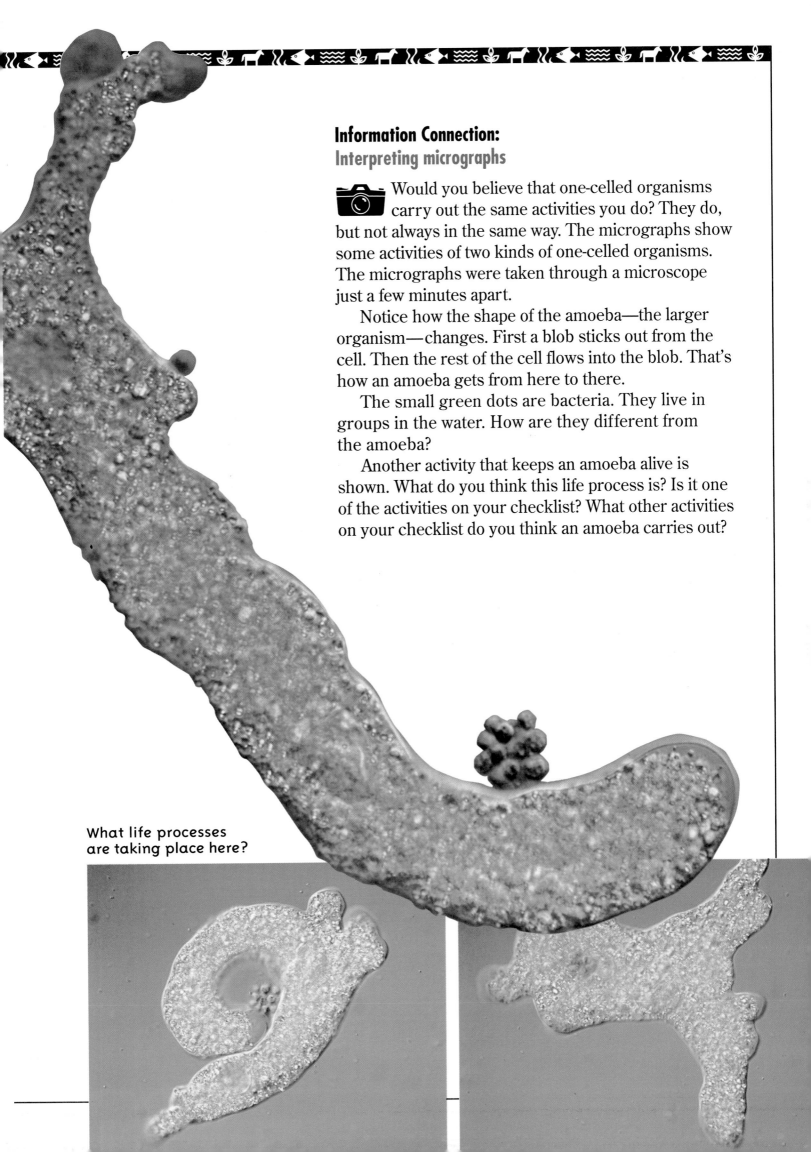

Information Connection:
Interpreting micrographs

Would you believe that one-celled organisms carry out the same activities you do? They do, but not always in the same way. The micrographs show some activities of two kinds of one-celled organisms. The micrographs were taken through a microscope just a few minutes apart.

Notice how the shape of the amoeba—the larger organism—changes. First a blob sticks out from the cell. Then the rest of the cell flows into the blob. That's how an amoeba gets from here to there.

The small green dots are bacteria. They live in groups in the water. How are they different from the amoeba?

Another activity that keeps an amoeba alive is shown. What do you think this life process is? Is it one of the activities on your checklist? What other activities on your checklist do you think an amoeba carries out?

What life processes are taking place here?

Look back at your checklist of life processes that you think all living things must do to stay alive. Because plants are living things, they carry out life processes. You can learn a lot about plants by growing them and observing them for a few weeks.

Exploration:
Plant some seeds.

You need:

Paper towels
Water
8 cups
Seeds
2 cardboard boxes
Lid for one box
Plastic wrap

❶ Crumple two paper towels and push them into one of the cups. Then pour water a little at a time onto the paper towels to make them damp but not soggy. Prepare the rest of the cups the same way.

❷ Put three seeds into each cup. Push the seeds halfway down the cup between the side of the cup and the damp towels.

❸ Place four cups in each box. Put the lid on one box. Stretch plastic wrap over the other box. Put the boxes near a window. Predict what will happen to the seeds in each box in two or three days.

❹ Observe the cups every day. Make a record of any changes you see in the seeds. Be sure to keep the towels damp.

❺ Compare your group's observations with the observations of the other groups.

Interpret your results.

• How did the seeds in the box with the lid grow compared with those in the box without the lid? Were your predictions about the seeds in the two boxes correct?

• What do you think young plants need in order to grow well?

Closer to Home:
Is a robot a living thing?

Have you ever seen a robot in a movie or on TV? If so, did it look like either of these robots? What kinds of things could the robot in the movie or on TV do that humans usually do?

Robots once existed only in fiction, but today they're a part of real life. They're machines, and most of them don't look anything like a human. But they can do many things that humans can do. Although most people don't have them in their homes, there are robots that can vacuum a room or serve food at a party. Using a robot to do a chore gives people more time to enjoy themselves or to do other work.

Robots do a lot of work in factories that people used to do. For example, they can weld, rivet, turn screws, drill, and apply paint.

Robots can go where people can't go, such as deep in the ocean. Those robots can collect samples of the ocean floor or capture organisms to be studied.

How can robots do so many things? Robots run on electricity. They're controlled by computers. They "see" with built-in television cameras and "feel" with electronic sensors.

- In what ways does a robot seem like a living thing?

- Why does a robot need a source of electricity? Why don't you need one?

- What are some things a robot can do that are like life processes?

- How do you know a robot isn't alive?

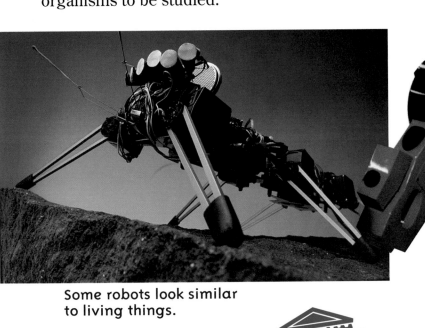
Some robots look similar to living things.

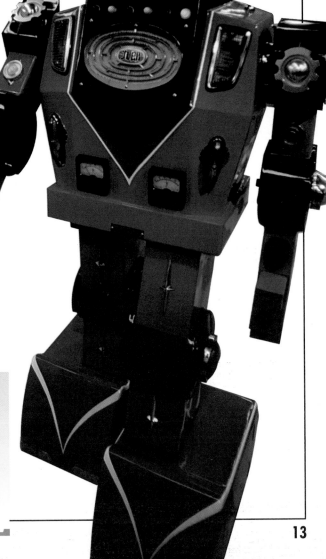

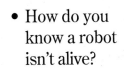
Think!

A dead organism is not the same thing as a nonliving thing. Explain why not.

How Do Plants Get Food?

Is eating one of the activities on your checklist? Getting food is one of the things you have to do to stay alive—it's a life process. All living things need food, but how they get it differs. You and an ameba certainly have different ways of getting food. What about plants? They're living things, so they need food. But plants don't eat. How do you think the plants growing from the seeds you planted get food?

Exploration:
Observe seedlings.

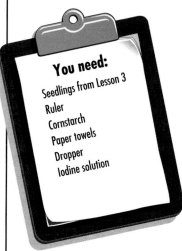

You need:
Seedlings from Lesson 3
Ruler
Cornstarch
Paper towels
Dropper
Iodine solution

❶ Observe the cups of seeds you planted in Lesson 3. Compare the plants grown in the two boxes.

❷ Measure the plants. Record your observations. ✎

❸ Put some cornstarch on a paper towel. With the dropper, put a drop of iodine solution on the cornstarch. If you notice a change in color, add one more drop of iodine and check the color again.

❹ With the dropper, put a drop of iodine solution on different parts of one of the seedlings grown in light.

❺ Repeat step 4 with one of the seedlings grown in the dark.

Interpret your results.

• Anything that contains starch will change color when iodine solution is added to it. In which parts of the seedling grown in light did you find starch? In which parts of the seedling grown in the dark did you find starch?

• Starch is food. What did you learn about the way plants get food?

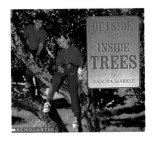

Exploration Connection:
Using reference books

Unlike many other living things, plants don't move around to get food. Instead, plants have a process called <u>photosynthesis</u>. The process is shown in the diagram. What materials does a plant need for photosynthesis?

How does a plant get each of these materials? What kind of energy do plants use in photosynthesis? Where do you think most of a plant's photosynthesis takes place? Turn to pages 17–19 of *Outside and Inside Trees* to find out more.

PHOTOSYNTHESIS

The green parts of a plant take in sunlight.

Carbon dioxide enters a leaf through tiny openings.

Leaf cells change sunlight, carbon dioxide, and water into sugar and oxygen.

Oxygen leaves a leaf.

The roots take in water.

How Plants Make and Use Food

When a plant makes its food—sugar—it doesn't use the food all at once. The plant changes the sugar it doesn't need right away into starch, which it stores to use later on. Many plants store the starch in their green leaves. Plants need food to stay alive, and they don't just need it during the day. Plants make food through a process called photosynthesis. The word *photosynthesis* means "the use of light to make something." At night, the plant can't make sugar, because there's no sunlight. Some stored starch is changed back into sugar, which travels through the plant to the parts of the plant that need food.

Starch isn't food just for plants. It's food for all kinds of animals, too. Whenever an animal eats a plant or part of a plant, the animal takes in sugar or starch that the plant made. Starch is one of the most important foods that animals eat. When an animal digests starch, its body converts the starch into energy. An organism's cells need energy to do their jobs. That means that every tissue, organ, and system requires energy to work.

If you were to try the iodine test you used in the Exploration on the foods you eat, you'd discover that some foods contain starch. **Try it!** Just <u>don't eat</u> any of the foods you test.

What other foods do you eat that might contain starch? Brainstorm with your class to come up with a list of foods to test, and try the iodine test on those foods.

▲ People eat both the fruit and the leaves of grape plants.

Closer to Home: Plants you eat

What plants or parts of plants did you have for breakfast today? Did you have orange juice? It came from the fruit produced by an orange tree. Does orange juice contain starch? How could you find out? **Try it!**

Besides starch, plants can make other food materials. Some plants make fats and oils. Some plants make proteins—the food we usually think of getting from animal products. Beans, for example, are rich in proteins.

You're growing taller every day. You're gaining weight, too. Where do you think the new material for your growing body comes from? Plants grow, too. Like you, plants turn food into new tissues as they grow. Plants also make new parts, such as leaves, flowers, fruit, and branches. They build new parts from sugars, fats, oils, and proteins. And they store food in different body parts.

- Potatoes and carrots grow underground. Where in a potato plant or carrot plant is food made? How do you think the food gets to the underground parts?

Most photosynthesis goes on in green leaves. Cactus leaves are sharp spines with very little space for food-making. Where in a cactus do you think food is made?

How Do Animals Get Food?

Most plants are rooted in one spot. You aren't. Plants are green and many make flowers. You aren't, and you can't. These are some big differences between you and plants, but there's another difference that's even bigger. Plants make their own food. That's something that neither you nor any other animal can do. How do you think a plant's ability to make its own food affects animals?

Plants use nonliving things—air, water, and light—to make food. Animals can't do that, and they can't survive by eating only nonliving things such as water. Where do animals get their food?

Look at the picture on these pages. Every arrow goes from one organism to another—from what is eaten to what eats it. Follow the arrow that leads to the mouse. The arrow shows what the mouse eats. How does the organism that serves as the mouse's food get its own food? Next, follow the arrow leading away from the mouse to find out what eats the mouse. These three organisms connected by the arrows are linked to each other in a <u>food chain</u>. Find the other food chains in the picture. What other food chains do you know about?

A food chain can be very long, but most food chains start with plants. That's because plants, using the sun's energy, make food. This food then passes along the food chain when some organism eats the plant. The second organism in a food chain is usually a plant eater, and the third organism is one that eats the plant eater.

Would you expect to find a plant in the middle of a food chain? Why or why not? Would a long food chain have more plant-eating animals or more meat-eating animals? Explain.

You're a part of many food chains. Think about what you ate for breakfast this morning, and see if you can make food chains for some of the foods you ate. If you had bacon, for example, your food chain might be corn → pig → me. You should hope you're the last organism in any of the food chains you're in. Why?

◄ What food chains are in this picture?

Information Connection:
Interpreting diagrams

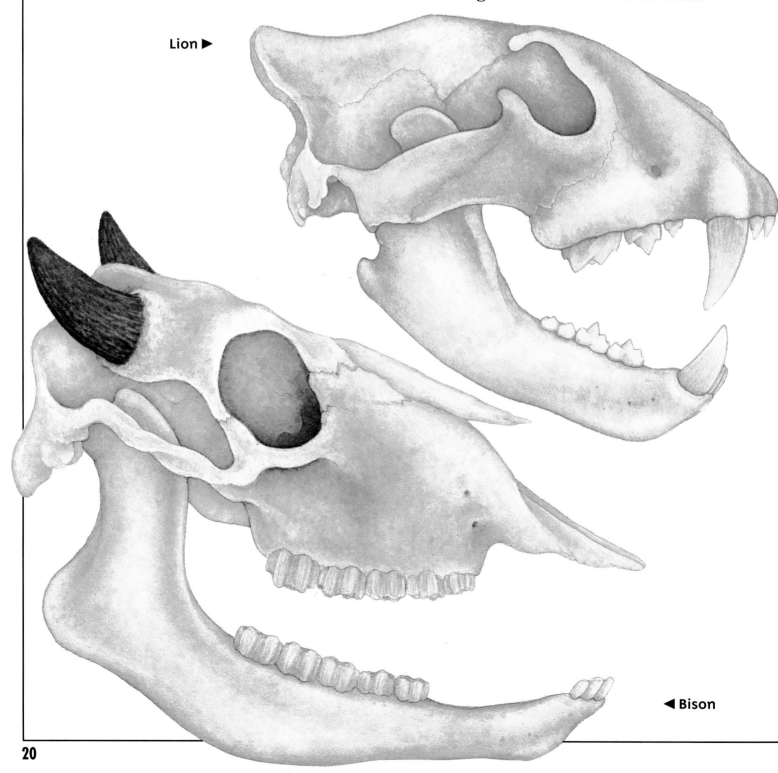

Animals that eat mainly plants or plant products—such as seeds and berries—are called <u>herbivores</u>. Animals that eat mainly meat are called <u>carnivores</u>.

You can tell what animals eat by observing their mouth parts. For example, you can tell what mammals eat by observing their teeth.

A meat-eating mammal has long, sharp, pointed teeth near the front of its mouth. With these teeth a carnivore can easily hold on to an animal and then tear out chunks of meat after it has been killed. Most herbivores have many wide, flat teeth that they use to grind their food. Leaves and stems of plants need lots of chewing.

Which diagram shows a carnivore's teeth? Which diagram shows a herbivore's teeth?

Lion ▶

◀ Bison

Closer to Home:
Food for you

You have to eat a variety of foods for your body to work properly and to stay healthy. You probably know you need many different vitamins. These are chemicals your body can't make. So you get most of the vitamins you need by eating different kinds of plants. You also need many different minerals, such as calcium and iron. You can get some minerals by eating vegetables and some by eating meat and animal products such as milk.

Although some people choose to eat only vegetables, humans are actually <u>omnivores</u>. Omnivores eat both plants and meat. Two omnivores are shown on pages 18 and 19. Which animals are they?

Just as you can tell a herbivore and a carnivore by their teeth, you can tell an omnivore by its teeth. Human teeth are shown in the diagram. How do they compare with the teeth of the herbivore and the carnivore shown on page 20? Which of the human teeth are like a herbivore's teeth? Which of the teeth are like a carnivore's teeth?

- A person who chooses not to eat meat or other animal products has to plan wisely to make sure his or her diet includes exactly the right kinds of vegetables. Why?

- How easy is it to eat celery or lettuce using just your front teeth? **Try it!**

Think!

If something were to prevent the sun's light from reaching Earth for a very long time, what do you think would happen to animals? Why?

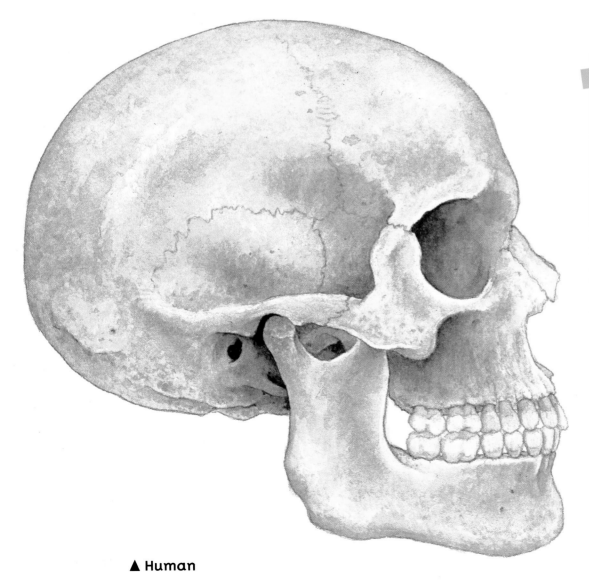

▲ Human

How Do Living Things Use Food?

Plants store some of the sun's energy in the food they make. When animals eat plants, they take in the food with its stored energy. They use some of the energy for carrying out life processes. They store some of the energy in their body tissues. They give off some energy as heat. Do you think all living things get energy from food?

Exploration:
Take yeast's temperature.

You need:

Spoon
Flour
3 cups
Measuring cup
Thermometer
Yeast
Tap water
Paper towels

❶ Put three heaping spoonfuls of flour into one cup.

❷ Put hot water in another cup. Check the water's temperature with the thermometer. Add cold or hot water to make it about 42° C. Quickly measure 30 cc of this warm water and add it a little at a time to the flour. Mix the flour and water with the spoon.

❸ Put a thermometer into the mixture. After a minute, record the temperature. Leave the thermometer in place. Record the temperature every 5 minutes for 25 minutes. Make a drawing to record how the mixture looks. ✎

❹ Put three heaping spoonfuls of flour in the third cup. Add one heaping spoonful of yeast and mix.

❺ Follow steps 2 and 3 using the flour-and-yeast mixture.

Interpret your results.

• How did the appearance of the two mixtures differ?

• How did the temperature of each mixture change?

• Flour is a food. Yeast is a living thing. What do you think was happening in the yeast cup?

• Would you have observed the same results if you had used only yeast and water? Why? **Try it!**

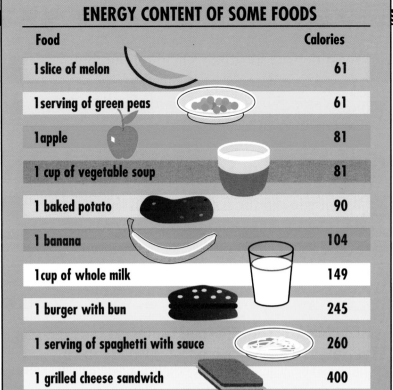

ENERGY CONTENT OF SOME FOODS

Food	Calories
1 slice of melon	61
1 serving of green peas	61
1 apple	81
1 cup of vegetable soup	81
1 baked potato	90
1 banana	104
1 cup of whole milk	149
1 burger with bun	245
1 serving of spaghetti with sauce	260
1 grilled cheese sandwich	400

▲ These plants melt the snow around them. Where does their heat come from?

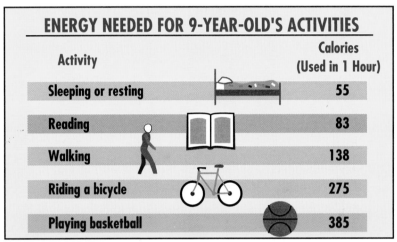

ENERGY NEEDED FOR 9-YEAR-OLD'S ACTIVITIES

Activity	Calories (Used in 1 Hour)
Sleeping or resting	55
Reading	83
Walking	138
Riding a bicycle	275
Playing basketball	385

Exploration Connection:
Interpreting tables

The number of Calories in a food describes how much energy your body can get from the food. Calories are also used to describe how much energy you use to live and carry out all your activities. Look at the tables. One of them shows the number of Calories in certain foods. The other shows how many Calories a person of your age uses when doing certain activities. Which has more Calories—a cup of whole milk or a banana and an apple together?

Suppose you'll have five hours of school, then a one-hour basketball game, and then you'll ride your bike for half an hour to get home. How many Calories will you use up? Using the foods listed, choose a lunch that will provide at least enough Calories for you to follow this schedule.

Yeast doesn't look like a living thing, but you found that it performs a life process, using its stored-up energy. Could you show that seeds have stored-up energy, too?

Energy Stored in Seeds

When you did the Exploration in this lesson, you used two setups: one with yeast, flour, and water, and one with flour and water. The second setup is called a control. Without a control, you can't be sure of the reason for any changes you observe.

The diagrams on this page show an experiment that uses a control. Two identical bottles each have wet cotton at the bottom. Both bottles are sealed tightly so that air can't get into or out of them. A thermometer reaches into each bottle so that the temperature inside each bottle can be measured. One of the bottles is nearly filled with seeds that are starting to grow. The other bottle—the one without seeds—is the control.

The first diagram shows the beginning of the experiment. The temperatures in the two bottles are the same—that's one of the conditions of having a controlled experiment. The second diagram shows what's happened after twelve hours. The temperature in the bottle with the seeds has risen; the temperature in the control has dropped. You can tell from the third diagram that the temperature difference is even greater after another twelve hours.

The experiment shows that the seeds' growth process releases energy—heat. They're performing a life process: using the energy they have stored in them.

Monday 10:00 a.m.

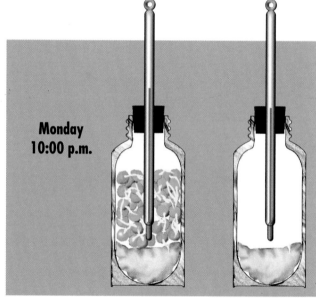

Monday 10:00 p.m.

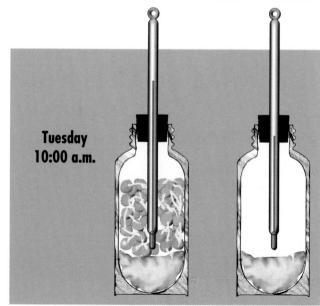

Tuesday 10:00 a.m.

Closer to Home:
Take a deep breath.

You couldn't live underwater or in outer space because you wouldn't be able to breathe there. What's so important about breathing?

You need oxygen to get energy from foods you've eaten. In fact, most living things need a constant supply of oxygen. That's because they're always using energy—even when they're asleep. You get oxygen from the air. Your blood carries the oxygen to your cells. Inside your cells, the oxygen combines with tiny bits of food, releasing the energy in the food for your cells' use. Each breath you take gives you enough oxygen to last until the next breath—but not much longer.

Suppose you and a friend raced each other to the corner. The graph shows how this exercise would change your breathing. Notice that the graph line begins to go up even before the exercise period begins. That rising line means that you would begin to breathe more deeply and rapidly before you began running. Then, as you started to race, you'd take even deeper and faster breaths.

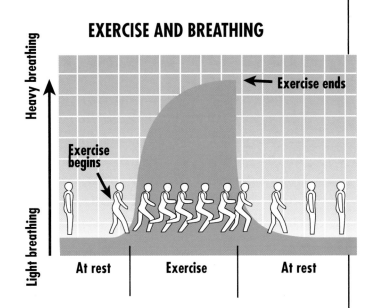

EXERCISE AND BREATHING

Heavy breathing

Light breathing

Exercise begins

Exercise ends

At rest   Exercise   At rest

The steeply rising graph line shows this. But then notice that the graph line levels off. That means you would be taking steady, rapid breaths. Now look at what happens to the graph line when the race ends. How would your breathing change?

• Why do you think your breathing changes even before you start exercising?

• After you've exercised hard, what do you notice about your body when you first stop exercising? How might this explain what the graph shows?

Think!

What is the original source of the energy that's in the food plants make? What is the original source of the energy that's in the food animals eat?

How Do Living Things Use Water?

You know why living things need food and oxygen. You probably also know that living things need water. But do you know why they need water? One reason you might think of is that plants use water in photosynthesis. That's a good answer—but you need water, too, and you don't make your own food. Which life processes do you think living things need water for?

Exploration:
Observe water in a plant.

You need:

2 cups
Water
Food coloring
Celery stalk with leaves
Plastic knife

❶ Fill each cup half full of water. Carefully add a few drops of food coloring to color the water in one of the cups. Stir with the knife.

❷ Cut the celery stalk so that it is about 15 cm long below the leaves. Then cut a slit about 10 cm long starting at the bottom of the stalk. Put one part of the stalk in each cup.

❸ Observe the celery every 3 or 4 minutes and record your observations. Stop after about 10 minutes. Check the stalk in another 20 minutes.

Interpret your results.

• What happened to the food coloring in the water? What do you think would happen to sugar in water? **Try it!**

• What changes did you observe in both parts of the celery stalk? Do you think that the uncolored water acted the same way as the colored water?

• Plants get the minerals they need from the water they take in from soil. How could the process you observed help the minerals move from one part of a plant to another?

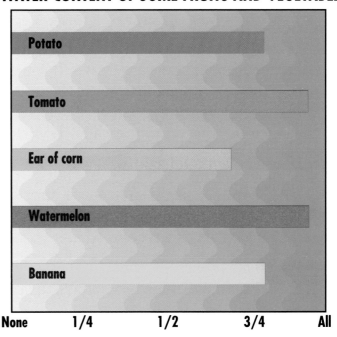

Plants lose large amounts of water through their leaves. Do you think a banana plant, like the one at the left, loses more or less water through its leaves than a mesquite plant, like the one above, loses? Explain.

Exploration Connection:
Interpreting graphs

You know two ways that plants use water. Plants lose a lot of water to the air around them through their leaves. They need to take in water to replace what they've lost.

There's more water in plants than you might think. In fact, many plants are mostly water. Think about the size of a grape and the size of a raisin. Raisins are dried grapes. How would you explain their size difference? Now look at the graph showing the water content of some fruits and vegetables. Which are more than 3/4 water?

WATER CONTENT OF SOME FRUITS AND VEGETABLES

Potato				
Tomato				
Ear of corn				
Watermelon				
Banana				
None	1/4	1/2	3/4	All

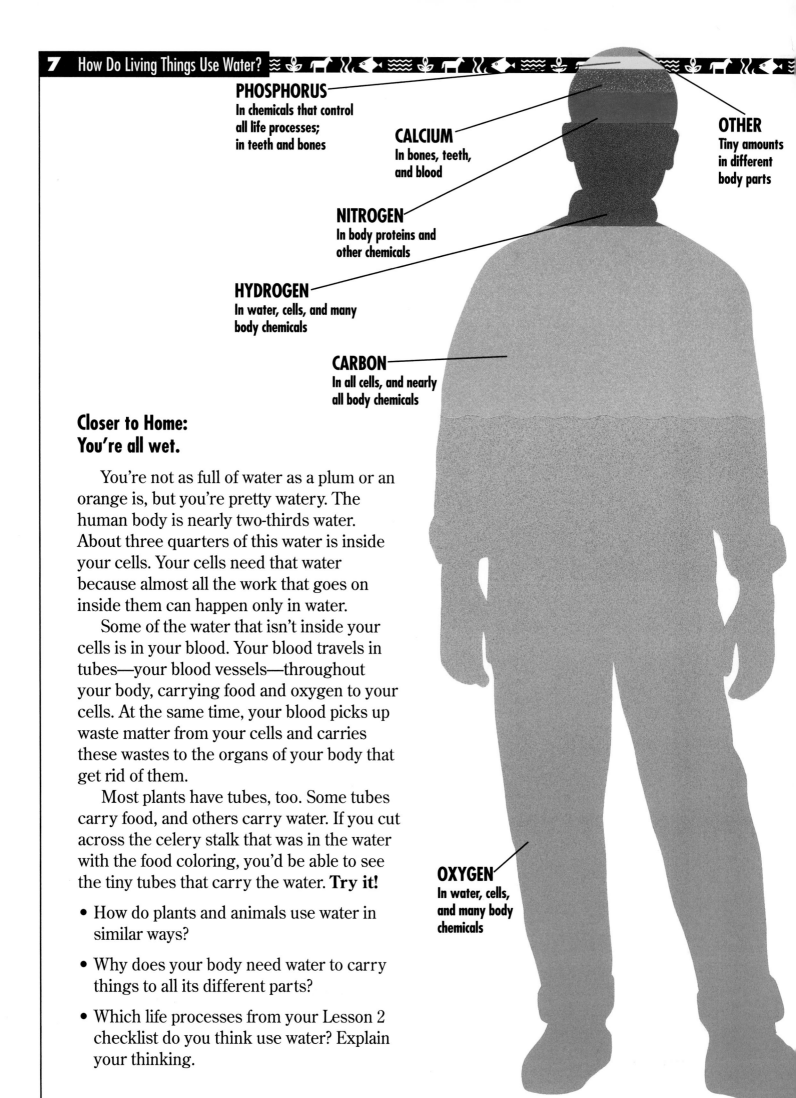

PHOSPHORUS
In chemicals that control
all life processes;
in teeth and bones

CALCIUM
In bones, teeth,
and blood

OTHER
Tiny amounts
in different
body parts

NITROGEN
In body proteins and
other chemicals

HYDROGEN
In water, cells, and many
body chemicals

CARBON
In all cells, and nearly
all body chemicals

OXYGEN
In water, cells,
and many body
chemicals

Closer to Home:
You're all wet.

You're not as full of water as a plum or an orange is, but you're pretty watery. The human body is nearly two-thirds water. About three quarters of this water is inside your cells. Your cells need that water because almost all the work that goes on inside them can happen only in water.

Some of the water that isn't inside your cells is in your blood. Your blood travels in tubes—your blood vessels—throughout your body, carrying food and oxygen to your cells. At the same time, your blood picks up waste matter from your cells and carries these wastes to the organs of your body that get rid of them.

Most plants have tubes, too. Some tubes carry food, and others carry water. If you cut across the celery stalk that was in the water with the food coloring, you'd be able to see the tiny tubes that carry the water. **Try it!**

- How do plants and animals use water in similar ways?

- Why does your body need water to carry things to all its different parts?

- Which life processes from your Lesson 2 checklist do you think use water? Explain your thinking.

WHAT YOUR BODY IS MADE OF

ALL OTHER MATERIALS

WATER

Think!

Some desert animals, such as the kangaroo rat, eat food but never drink. They have to have water. How do you think they get it?

What's Left Over When Cells Use Food?

When you take in enough food, oxygen, and water, all your cells can get the energy they need. When oxygen acts on food bits in your cells, energy in the food is released and some things your cells can't use are formed. These unwanted materials are wastes your body gets rid of. How do you think these cell wastes leave your body?

Exploration:
Investigate your breath.

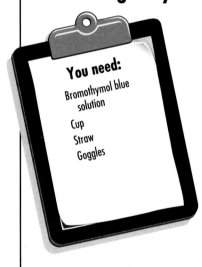

You need:

Bromothymol blue solution

Cup

Straw

Goggles

❶ Your teacher will pour some bromothymol blue solution into your cup.

❷ Use the straw to blow into the solution. Do *not* suck in!

❸ Look for a change in the solution, and keep blowing until you see the change.

❹ Compare your observations with the observations of the others in your group.

Interpret your results.

• What change did you observe in the solution when you breathed into it?

• Carbon dioxide turns bromothymol blue solution yellow. What do you know about the air you breathe out?

BROMOTHYMOL BLUE

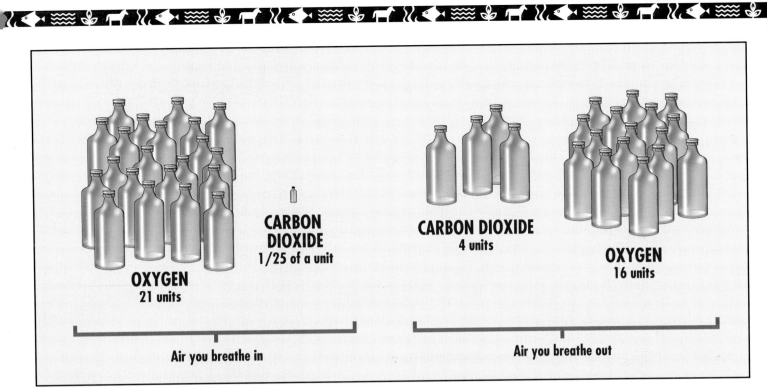

CARBON DIOXIDE
1/25 of a unit

OXYGEN
21 units

Air you breathe in

CARBON DIOXIDE
4 units

OXYGEN
16 units

Air you breathe out

▲ Oxygen and carbon dioxide in 100 units of air. Why do the changes between the air you breathe in and the air you breathe out occur?

Exploration Connection:
Interpreting diagrams

When oxygen acts on food bits in your cells and releases energy, carbon dioxide forms. Too much of this gas in your cells would poison them, so your body gets rid of the carbon dioxide.

The diagram shows the amounts of oxygen and carbon dioxide in the air you take in and the air you breathe out. Is there more oxygen in the air you breathe in or the air you breathe out? What is the reason for this difference? Is there more carbon dioxide in the air you breathe in or the air you breathe out? Explain.

You know that your cells always have a lot of water. But extra water is a waste, just as carbon dioxide is. Most extra water leaves your body in urine. But some leaves your body as the gas called water vapor.

Waste water can also leave your body the same way carbon dioxide does. Hold a mirror in front of your mouth and breathe onto it. Does the mirror fog up the way the bathroom mirror does when you take a warm shower or bath? **Try it!** Fog forms when water vapor turns back to liquid water. Where is the water vapor coming from?

You've discovered that your cells need to combine oxygen with food to release energy and that your cells produce carbon dioxide as a waste. You get rid of carbon dioxide when you breathe out. You also know that plants use carbon dioxide to make sugar. In that process, plants give off oxygen as a waste. What do you think plants use with their food to produce the energy they need?

Plant Waste

When night falls, a plant doesn't just stop performing all of its life processes. If it did, it would die. The plant uses some of the food it stored as starch for the energy it needs to stay alive. (In fact, the plant has to use its food during the day, too.) Both plants and animals need to combine oxygen and food to produce energy. Both plants and animals also produce carbon dioxide as a waste.

At night, the plant gets the oxygen from the same place as you do—the air. You rely on your lungs to take in oxygen from the air. A plant takes in oxygen from the air surrounding its leaves. Most of the oxygen enters the plant through tiny holes on the undersides of the leaves. (That's also where the plant releases most of its carbon dioxide waste.) The oxygen travels through tiny air spaces in the leaf, until it reaches the plant cells.

In all animals and plants, oxygen can't reach the inside of a cell unless it's dissolved in a liquid. A fish's gills take in oxygen that's already dissolved in liquid. When you breathe in, oxygen dissolves in a liquid on the inside surfaces of your lungs. In plants, oxygen dissolves in a liquid that covers the cells.

As you would expect, the more energy a plant needs, the more oxygen it needs. Plants generally use the most oxygen—and produce the most carbon dioxide—in the spring. Can you figure out why?

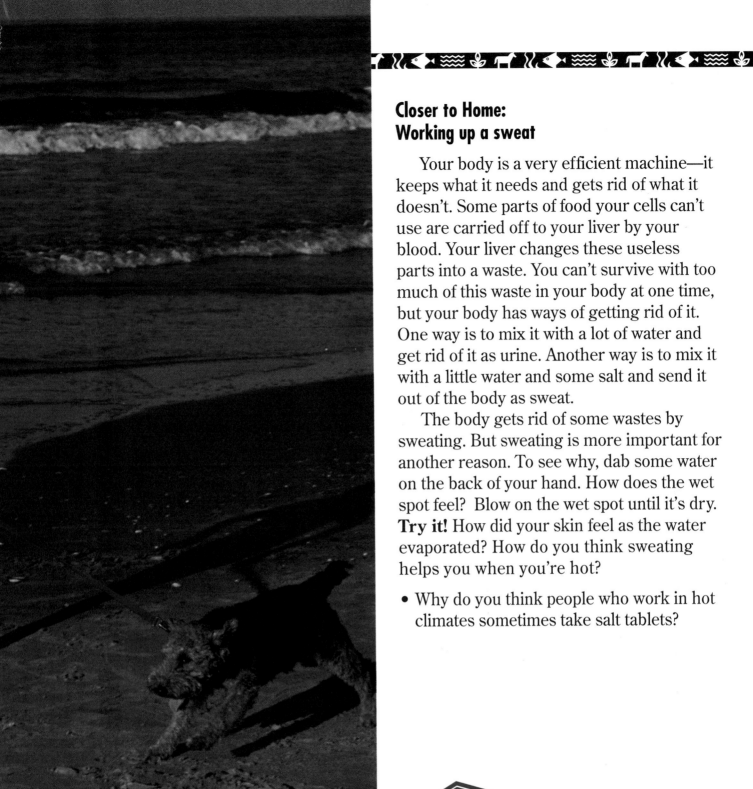

Closer to Home: Working up a sweat

Your body is a very efficient machine—it keeps what it needs and gets rid of what it doesn't. Some parts of food your cells can't use are carried off to your liver by your blood. Your liver changes these useless parts into a waste. You can't survive with too much of this waste in your body at one time, but your body has ways of getting rid of it. One way is to mix it with a lot of water and get rid of it as urine. Another way is to mix it with a little water and some salt and send it out of the body as sweat.

The body gets rid of some wastes by sweating. But sweating is more important for another reason. To see why, dab some water on the back of your hand. How does the wet spot feel? Blow on the wet spot until it's dry. **Try it!** How did your skin feel as the water evaporated? How do you think sweating helps you when you're hot?

- Why do you think people who work in hot climates sometimes take salt tablets?

▲ Sweating helps to cool you. You have sweat glands all over your body. A dog has few sweat glands, all on the bottom of its feet. How do you think a dog cools off?

Exercising too much in hot weather can cause heatstroke. A person suffering from heatstroke can't sweat. Why is heatstroke dangerous?

How Do Living Things Grow?

Growing is another life process. Growth can take place when cells get the food, water, and other materials they need. How do you think cells make an organism grow?

Exploration:
Observe growing plants.

You need:
Tissues or paper towels
Plastic cup
4 seeds
Water
Ruler

❶ Crumple two paper towels and push them into the cup. Then pour a little water onto the towels to make them damp.

❷ Place four seeds in the cup. Push the seeds about halfway down, between the damp paper and the side of the cup.

❸ Predict which part of the seedling will sprout first—roots, stem, or leaves.

❹ After the seeds sprout, measure the length of the seedlings each day for 10 days. Record your results. ✎

Interpret your results.

• When your seeds began to grow, which part of the seedling appeared first? How does sprouting this way help a plant to survive?

• When your plants started growing, they were made of a certain number of cells. What do you think happened to the number of cells as the plant grew larger?

◄ Tree's growth rings

Exploration Connection:
Using reference books

A plant grows as its cells divide. One cell divides into two cells. Each of these new cells can divide into two more cells. The trunk of a tree grows thicker when cells divide and add layers of new cells to the trunk, just under the bark.

The photograph shows a slice of a tree trunk. Each ring is made by one year's growth of the trunk. Each ring has a light part and a dark part. How do these rings form? Find out by turning to pages 8–10 of *Outside and Inside Trees*.

You can tell the age of a tree by counting the rings. Start with the oldest ring. Where is it? How old was this tree when it was cut?

The width of the rings tells what the weather was like when the rings were made. A narrow ring means the weather was dry that year. How old was the tree in the photograph in the wettest year of its life? in the driest year?

The sneakers of a two-year-old child and a nine-year-old child

Closer to Home:
How fast are you growing?

Like a tree, you grow faster at some times and more slowly at other times. Did your seedlings seem to grow faster and slower at different times? Explain.

Some of your fastest growth happened just before you were born. In the last two months before your birth, you probably grew 10 centimeters (4 inches) and gained more than 2 kilograms (about 5 pounds). After you were born and until you were two years old, you continued to grow very fast. Then your growth slowed down. But you're still growing and you'll keep on growing for many more years. At some time during those years, you'll go through another time of fast growth as your body changes from a child's body to an adult's body.

At times, some parts of your body grow more quickly than others. When you were a baby, your head was one fourth of your whole length. Your head was also bigger around than your chest. But as you got older, your head didn't grow as fast as the rest of your body. The length of an adult's head is only one eighth of the adult's total height.

Do you sometimes think you can see your hair grow? Your hair will keep growing all through your life. Each hair you can see on your head is made of dead cells. But each hair also has a living part. This living part is inside the skin of your scalp. The cells that make up this living, buried part of the hair divide. As the new hair cells form, the older hair cells are pushed toward the surface of the skin. They die before they get there, but new cells keep forming and pushing the dead cells along until they become the hair you can see.

Your fingernails also grow when their cells divide. The dividing cells are in the light-colored part at the bottom of the nail. There's more of this growing area that you can't see. It's underneath the skin at the bottom of the nail. As new nail cells form, they push the older ones to the tip of the nail. These cells and all the others on the upper layers of your nails are dead.

- How is the way you grow similar to the way your seedlings are growing?

Think!

How is your growth different from a plant's growth?

How Does Growth Help Plants Respond to Their Environments?

When a plant gets enough light and the materials it needs for photosynthesis, the plant can grow. When you think about the seedlings you've grown, you know that growth is not just getting bigger. Growth in plants means that new plant parts appear. How does each part help the new plant stay alive in its environment?

Exploration:

Observe how a plant gets light.

You need:

Scissors
2 boxes
Seedlings from Lesson 9
Pencil

❶ Use the scissors to cut a slit in the side of one box.

❷ Get two cups with the seedlings that started growing in Lesson 9. Water the seedlings if the paper in the cups is not damp. Then place one cup with seedlings under the box with a slit. Place the other cup under the other box.

❸ After one day, pick up the boxes. Observe how the seedlings have grown. Draw the seedlings in both boxes. ✏

Interpret your results.

• In which direction did the seedlings under the box with a slit grow? the seedlings in the other box?

• Why do you think the plants in the two boxes grew in different directions?

• How do you think the way a plant grows helps it to survive?

Exploration Connection:
Interpreting tables

Trees A and B are the same kind of tree and are the same age. Tree A is growing at the edge of the woods. Tree B is growing in the middle of the woods with other trees all around it. The measurements of the trees are given in the table.

Which tree is taller? Which tree has a thicker trunk? Think about your Exploration. Why do you think one tree grew taller and the other grew a thicker trunk?

Growth of Two Trees

Diameter of trunk	A	Height of tree
98 cm (38 in.)		8 m (26 ft)
45 cm (18 in.)	B	12 m (39 ft)

You've seen what a plant does when it needs more light. What are some other ways a plant responds to its environment?

Exploration:
Observe other plant responses.

You need:
Seedlings from Lesson 9
Pencil
Marker

❶ Observe how the seedlings from Lesson 9 have grown. Make a drawing of each seedling. Include all parts of the plants.

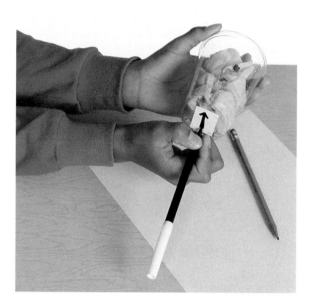

❷ Add water if needed to make the paper in the cup damp. Then lay the cup on its side near a window or a lamp. Draw an arrow on the bottom of the cup. The point of the arrow should be aimed at your classroom ceiling.

❸ After one day, observe each seedling. Record any changes in the way they're growing.

❹ Put the cup back on its side with the arrow pointing up. Check the cup every day for changes in the growth of the seedlings. Keep the paper damp.

Interpret your results.

• In which direction did the green part of the plants grow while the cup was on its side?

• Which way did the roots grow?

• How do you think growing in the ways you have observed helps plants survive?

• In what direction do you predict the plants would grow if you turned the cup right-side-up again? **Try it!**

▶ A commercial greenhouse

Closer to Home:
Keeping plants in line

Do you have potted plants in your home or classroom? What do you do to keep the plants from growing in only one direction? Most plants are prettier when they get sunlight evenly on all sides.

Many of the plants that people buy for their homes are grown in greenhouses. Greenhouses are buildings in which the walls and roof are made of glass or clear plastic. The glass or plastic lets in lots of light. Everything inside a greenhouse can be controlled to make it a healthy place for plants to grow. The temperature can be changed to suit the plants' needs. So can the amount of moisture in the air. If you've ever visited a greenhouse, you probably thought it was a fine place for plants to live—but too hot and humid for you.

▶ These plants are growing in a rainy city, but their natural home is in the desert. How can they survive here?

- Plants in greenhouses usually don't grow lopsided. How do you think the plants get light evenly?

- What other advantages can you think of for growing plants in greenhouses?

Think!

When you plant seeds for a garden, do you think it matters which end or side of the seed points up toward the surface of the soil? Explain your answer.

41

How Do Animals Respond to Their Environments?

Animals can respond to their environments much more rapidly than plants usually can. If an animal senses danger, it can run away. Many animals travel great distances to find an environment with the right conditions. What are some of these conditions?

Exploration:
Observe sow bug behavior.

You need:

Pan
White paper
Black paper
Tape
Sow bugs
Paper towels
Dropper
Water

❶ Cover one half of the bottom of a pan with white paper and the other half with black paper. Tape the edges down.

❷ Place five sow bugs in the pan. Handle them gently.

❸ After five minutes, count the sow bugs on each piece of paper. Record your results. ✏

❹ Remove the paper and the sow bugs—gently—from the pan. Now put two pieces of paper towel in the pan. Use the dropper to add a few drops of water to one of the pieces until it is damp but not soggy.

❺ Place five sow bugs in the pan.

❻ After five minutes, count the sow bugs on each piece of paper. Record your results. ✏

Interpret your results.

• How do you think sow bugs respond to dark and light?

• How do the sow bugs respond to wet and dry areas?

• What kind of environment do you think a sow bug needs in order to survive?

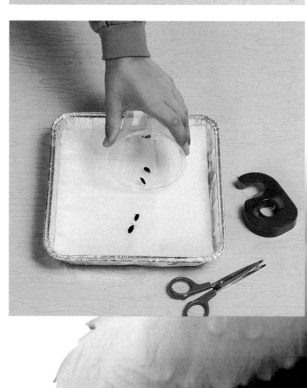

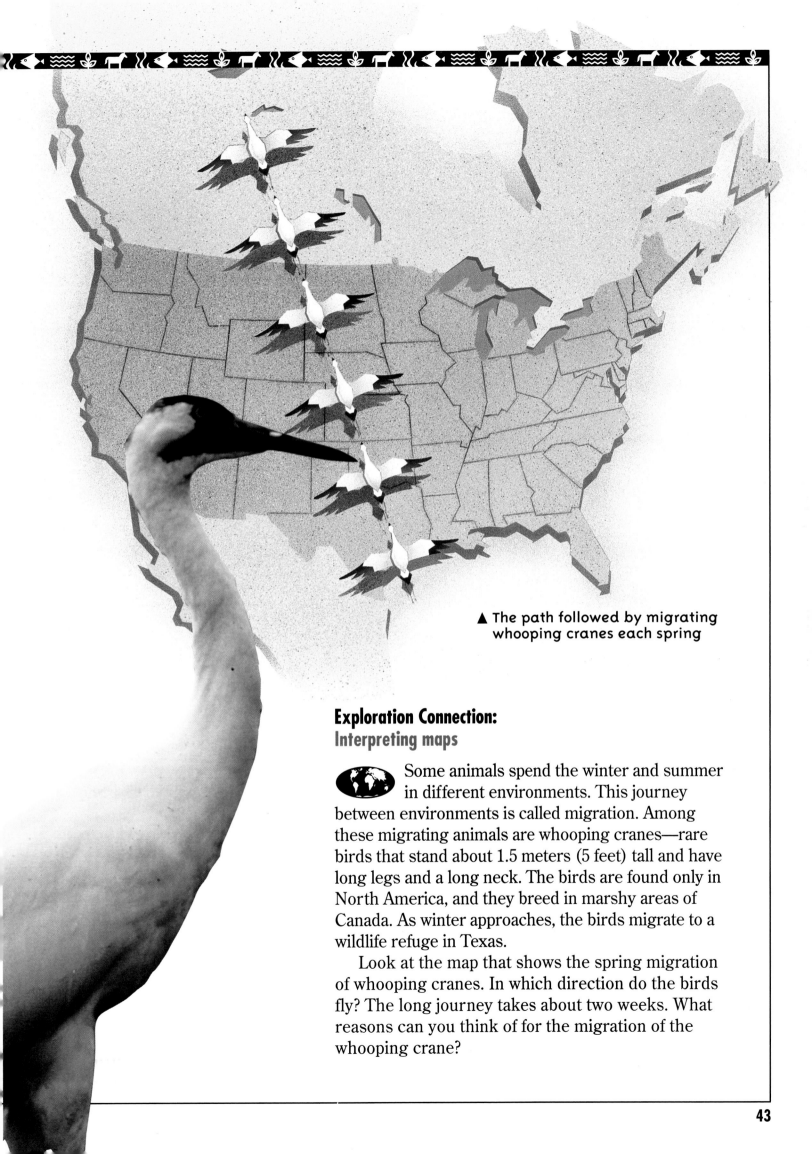

▲ The path followed by migrating whooping cranes each spring

Exploration Connection:
Interpreting maps

Some animals spend the winter and summer in different environments. This journey between environments is called migration. Among these migrating animals are whooping cranes—rare birds that stand about 1.5 meters (5 feet) tall and have long legs and a long neck. The birds are found only in North America, and they breed in marshy areas of Canada. As winter approaches, the birds migrate to a wildlife refuge in Texas.

Look at the map that shows the spring migration of whooping cranes. In which direction do the birds fly? The long journey takes about two weeks. What reasons can you think of for the migration of the whooping crane?

▲ A young white-tailed deer

Closer to Home:
Animals respond to you.

Animals respond to light, temperature, moisture, smell, taste, and other things in their environment. But did you ever think that animals also respond to you? When you try to hit a fly, it moves away from you as quickly as it can. Tiny hairs cover its body. Some of the hairs are so sensitive that even a gentle air current will bend them. No matter how carefully you move your hand toward a fly, the insect will dart off almost every time. Its hairs warn the fly that the air around it is being moved.

Sometimes an animal's response is not to get away from you but to go toward you. A mosquito, for example, moves toward you in order to find a meal.

You learned in Lesson 8 that you give off carbon dioxide as a waste when you breathe out. A mosquito can find you by detecting that carbon dioxide. If you've ever tried to get rid of a pesky mosquito, you know how attracted to humans they are.

Instead of going toward or away from humans, some animals stay right where they are. Many animals respond to humans—and to other animals that might be enemies—by not moving. They can be as still as statues. Rabbits often do this instead of running away from danger. Some animals go even further—they pretend to be dead when they're frightened. The opossum is the best known of these animal actors.

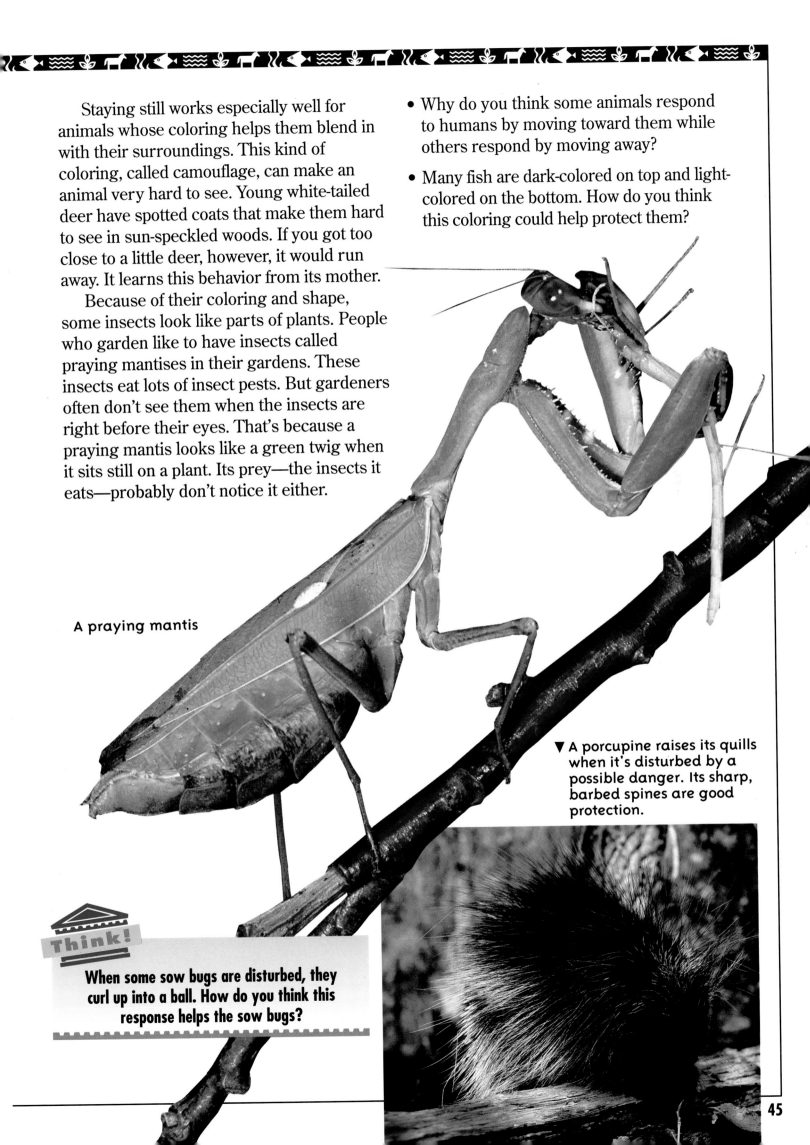

Staying still works especially well for animals whose coloring helps them blend in with their surroundings. This kind of coloring, called camouflage, can make an animal very hard to see. Young white-tailed deer have spotted coats that make them hard to see in sun-speckled woods. If you got too close to a little deer, however, it would run away. It learns this behavior from its mother.

Because of their coloring and shape, some insects look like parts of plants. People who garden like to have insects called praying mantises in their gardens. These insects eat lots of insect pests. But gardeners often don't see them when the insects are right before their eyes. That's because a praying mantis looks like a green twig when it sits still on a plant. Its prey—the insects it eats—probably don't notice it either.

- Why do you think some animals respond to humans by moving toward them while others respond by moving away?

- Many fish are dark-colored on top and light-colored on the bottom. How do you think this coloring could help protect them?

A praying mantis

▼ A porcupine raises its quills when it's disturbed by a possible danger. Its sharp, barbed spines are good protection.

Think!

When some sow bugs are disturbed, they curl up into a ball. How do you think this response helps the sow bugs?

45

How Do Plants and Animals Change During Their Lives?

Living things have a lot in common. They all perform similar life processes, and they all respond to their environments. Another thing plants and animals have in common is that they change.

When plants and animals are mature—when they're adults—they can reproduce. Look at the life cycles on this page and the next. Find the egg in each life cycle. What does each egg develop into? Now find the adult in each life cycle. The adult keeps the cycle going by making more of its own kind.

Look at the life cycle of the radish plant. How is the seedling like the adult plant? How is it different? The little leaves on the seedling are called seed leaves. They contain stored food for the plant to live on until true leaves can develop. True leaves can carry out photosynthesis. Then the plant can make its own food.

The form of a horse doesn't change very much as a newborn horse—called a foal—develops and becomes an adult. The foal and the adult horse have the same shape. They have the same number of legs. All their body parts are arranged in the same way. But there are some differences between them. Which ones can you see?

When a sow bug hatches from an egg, it's called a larva. How is it different from an adult sow bug? To grow, a sow bug has to first shed its hard covering. Then it grows a new hard covering. It does this several times before it reaches its adult size.

Seedling

Sprouting seed

LIFE CYCLE OF A RADISH

Egg

Hen

Chick

LIFE CYCLE OF A CHICKEN

Egg

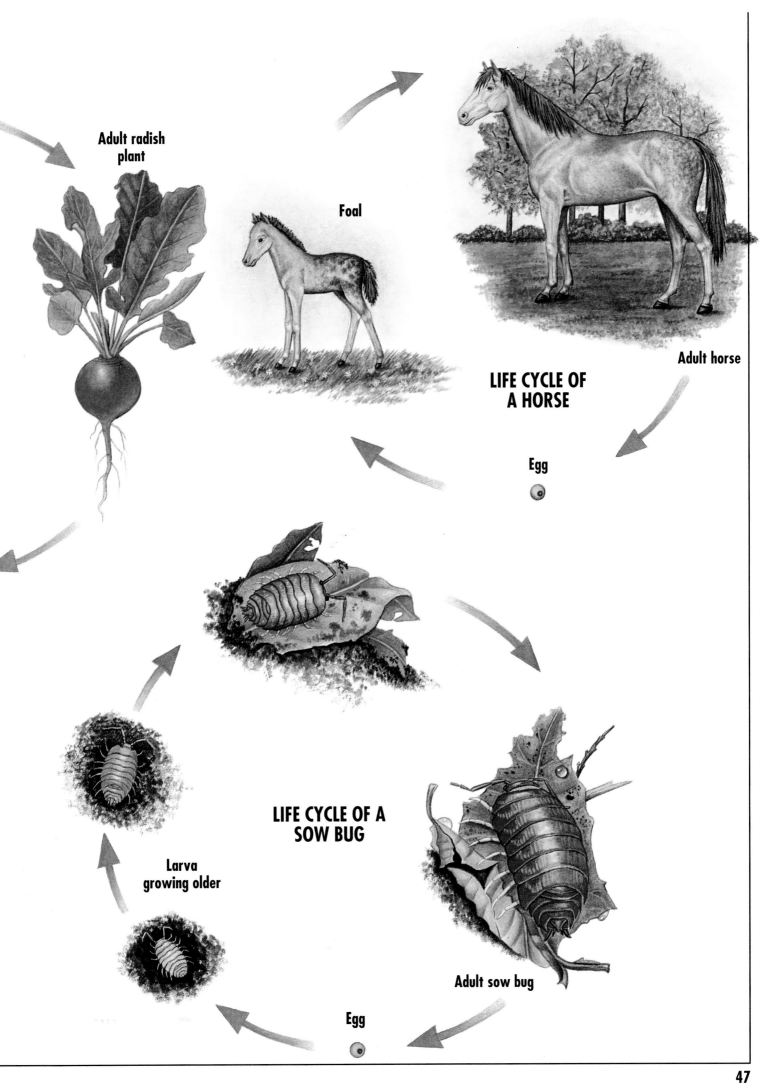

Adult radish
plant

Foal

**LIFE CYCLE OF
A HORSE**

Adult horse

Egg

**LIFE CYCLE OF A
SOW BUG**

Larva
growing older

Adult sow bug

Egg

METAMORPHOSIS OF A MOTH

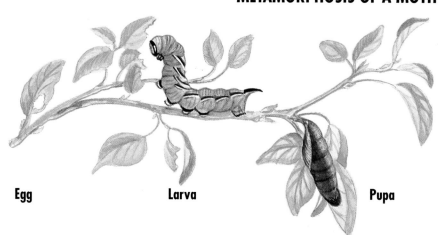

Egg   **Larva**   **Pupa**   **Moth**

METAMORPHOSIS OF A FROG

Mass of eggs   **Tadpole growing older**   **Frog**

▼ This drawing shows how the same two people might look at different times of their lives. The average length of life in the United States today is 75 years. In 1815 it was only 39 years. Why do you think this increase has come about?

Information Connection:
Using reference books

Some animals go through amazing changes as they grow from an egg to an adult. These changes are called <u>metamorphosis</u>. Some insects change the same way a sow bug does. Other insects go through the stages shown in the top diagram.

Frogs and toads also go through metamorphosis. What changes can you see taking place during the tadpole stage of a frog's metamorphosis?

Some animals change even when they're adults. Mammals that live where winters are cold often grow thicker coats for the winter. They shed the extra hair in spring. Do you think adult plants might change, too? You can find out by reading page 18 of *Flowers Trees & Other Plants*.

Closer to Home:
Changes and you

You're a living thing—so you change, too. In fact, you've already changed a lot. You're more than twice as tall as you were when you were a baby.

As you've grown, you've also learned new facts and ideas. When you were about 18 months old you may have known 20 words, and you probably used them only a word or two at a time. By the time you were 3 years old, you probably knew nearly 1,000 words, and you could put words together as sentences. Every year you're learning new things. Some things that you couldn't understand when you were 6 years old seem obvious to you now.

You don't get better at everything as you get older. Teachers have found that children can learn a lot of things—foreign languages, for example—faster than adults can. And if you want to compete as a gymnast or ballet dancer, the earlier you start training, the better your chances will be.

You're going to change a lot during your life. What other changes do you expect will happen to you?

• How are you similar to people younger than you? How are you different?

• How are you similar to people older than you? How are you different?

Think!

A corn plant lives four to six months. Some giant sequoia trees have lived more than two thousand years. Do you think the life cycle of a corn plant has the same stages as the life cycle of a giant sequoia tree? What would be the stages of each life cycle?

How Does a New Life Cycle Begin?

As organisms grow older, they change in ways that make it possible for them to make new living things of their own kind. Bacteria and other one-celled organisms, such as amebas, do this by dividing. One ameba becomes two. For organisms made of many cells, reproduction is more complicated. It takes specialized parts to produce a new organism with many cells.

Exploration:
Observe seed parts.

You need:

2 lima beans
Paper towels
Water
3 small plastic bags

❶ Look closely at the beans, which are actually seeds from a lima bean plant. Carefully peel off the thin outer skin from each bean.

❷ With your fingernails, carefully pry apart one of the beans so it splits into two halves. Make a sketch of each half.

❸ Dampen two pieces of paper towel and put each in a separate plastic bag. Place one lima bean half in each bag. The lima bean half should touch the wet paper in the bag.

❹ Prepare a third plastic bag the same way. Put a whole lima bean inside this bag.

❺ The next day, open the bags and inspect the beans.

Interpret your results.

• How are the two halves of a lima bean different?

• Which plastic bags contained sprouting bean plants after one day?

• Which half of the lima bean do you think is more important for making a new plant?

PARTS OF A FLOWER

Exploration Connection: Using reference books

Flowers are not just colorful decorations. They're the plant parts that make seeds.

The diagram shows the parts of a flower. Find the part that makes pollen and the part that makes eggs.

When it lands on the top of the pistil, a pollen grain sprouts a little tube that grows down into the ovary. There it joins with an egg, and a seed begins to form.

Some flowers need help in getting pollen to a pistil. What help do you think they can get? You can find out by reading page 11 of *Flowers, Trees & Other Plants*.

Seeds grow inside the ovary. The rest of the flower dries up and falls off the plant. The ovary with the seeds inside develops into a fruit, but you know some fruits as vegetables. Nuts, tomatoes, and peppers are fruits.

Ovary
The ovary is the part of the pistil that produces eggs.

Pistil
The top of the pistil is sticky and catches pollen grains.

Anther
The anther is the part of the stamen that makes pollen.

Stamen

You know that many plants grow from seeds. However, many of the same plants can produce new plants without using seeds. How could this happen?

Plants That Don't Come From Seeds

It's amazing that a new plant can grow from a seed, but there's another plant process that's even more astonishing. Under the right conditions, a new plant can grow from only a piece of a plant. The piece will form the other parts of the plant. This process is called vegetative propagation.

Vegetative propagation is common with plants such as strawberries, which have stems that run along the ground. Roots grow from these stems and form new plants. If you separate one of the new strawberry plants from the parent plant, the new plant will be a complete living organism.

Vegetative propagation is also common with plants that have bulbs, such as tulips or onions. A bulb is actually a kind of underground stem. A new plant will grow from a tulip bulb much faster than it will grow from a tulip seed. You could place an onion in a paper cup with water covering the bottom of the bulb, and the onion would sprout within a few days. **Try it!** New bulbs grow from the base of an older bulb.

Farmers use this process for growing new plants because it's fast and also because the new plant will be identical to the old one. A strong, healthy parent plant will produce new plants that are likely to be strong and healthy. How else might this be an advantage over growing from seeds? The process can be used for potatoes, apples, and many other plants. Farmers cut potatoes into small pieces and use the pieces to start new potato plants.

Apple trees are hardly ever grown from seeds, because vegetative propagation is faster and more successful. Instead, young branches from an apple tree are carefully attached to the trunk of an older tree, and the young branches become part of the older tree.

Farmers also cover the low branches of some plants with mounds of soil. The covered branches grow roots into the soil. When the rooted branches are cut off, they are individual living organisms.

▲ A rice paddy

▲ A wheat field

Closer to Home:
Seed food

When a plant first sprouts from a seed, it needs plenty of food to grow. But it hasn't yet had the chance to make its own food by photosynthesis. So when a parent plant makes a seed, it packs in a good supply of food.

As a baby plant begins to form inside the seed, it uses some of this stored food. It stores the rest of the food in some special leaves called seed leaves. Some flowering plants have one seed leaf; others have two. When the seedling grows out of the seed, it uses the food in the seed leaves until its true leaves develop. True leaves can carry out photosynthesis. The seed leaves, with most of their stored food used up, soon fall off.

Seeds are so full of food they're used as food by many animals, including humans. Lots of the foods you eat are cooked seeds, including rice, corn, beans, and peas.

Wheat is a seed that you usually eat in the form of bread or pasta. Wheat growers in the United States produced more than 55 million metric tons of wheat in one recent year. That's enough to supply every person in the country with about 214 kilograms (440 pounds) of wheat.

• What kinds of seeds have you eaten today?

Think!

Which part of a lima bean is food for the sprouting plant?

How Does a Species Survive?

All living things belong to groups called <u>species</u>. You and your friends belong to one particular species. So do all human beings. As long as at least one member of a species is alive, the species continues to exist. But when all the members of a species have died, the species is finished. What is the only way a species can continue to exist?

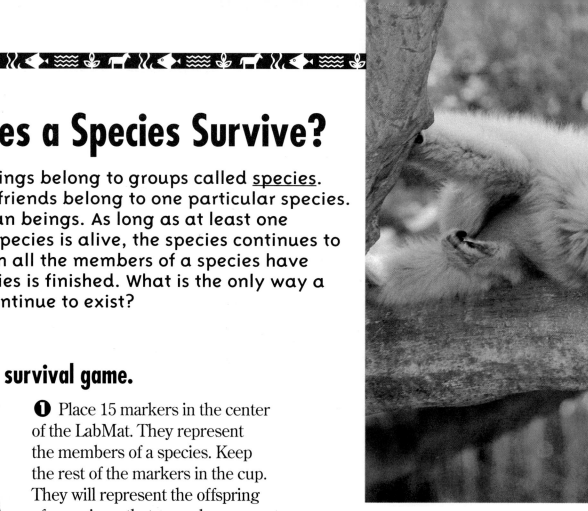

▲ Gibbons live in family groups for years. Here's a mother and her young.

Exploration:
Play a species survival game.

You need:
30 dried beans or other small markers
LabMat 14
Cup
Coin
Number cube

❶ Place 15 markers in the center of the LabMat. They represent the members of a species. Keep the rest of the markers in the cup. They will represent the offspring of organisms that reproduce.

❷ Place the coin on Square 1 of the LabMat and roll the number cube.

❸ Move the coin the number of spaces shown on the cube. If there are instructions on the space where you land, follow them.

❹ Keep rolling the number cube and moving the coin until there are no markers left on the LabMat, or until there are no markers left in the cup.

Interpret your results.

• What happens to a species if more members of the species are born than die?

• What happens to a species if more members of the species die than are born?

• What have you learned about how a species survives?

Exploration Connection:
Using reference books

How many children can a human being have in one year? Usually mothers give birth to one baby at a time. Human parents feed and protect their children for many years. Which animals in the table probably take care of their young? How can you tell?

As soon as they've laid their eggs, most parent fish leave them. Most of the eggs don't hatch. After the eggs that do survive hatch, the new little fish also have a hard time staying alive. The large number of eggs laid helps keep the species alive.

One of the fish in the table builds a nest for its eggs. The male guards the eggs until they hatch. Then he stays with the offspring for a few days. Which fish do you think this is ?

Plants such as dandelions produce large numbers of seeds, too. Usually only some of the seeds survive and grow into new plants. Even so, some kinds of plants have survived for more than 200 million years. Find out about these and other ancient plants by reading pages 36–37 of *Flowers, Trees & Other Plants*.

OFFSPRING PRODUCED IN 1 YEAR

Animal		Number
Codfish		9,000,000 (nine million)
Sea star		1,000,000 (one million)
Herring		50,000
Salmon		4,000
Stickleback		75-100
House mouse		25
Pigeon		10
Deer		1-2
Elephant		1 every 5 years

▶ After burying her eggs in the sand, this sea turtle will leave them alone.

Closer to Home: Saving species

If you've ever visited a zoo, you've probably seen at least one species of animal that may not be around much longer. Many zoos try to protect endangered species—those with few members left on the earth. For these animals, the number of births and deaths is not part of a game played with dried beans. If the number of new members of the species isn't larger than the number of members that die, the species will become extinct. A species becomes extinct when the last member of the species dies.

The whooping crane you learned about in Lesson 11 is a famous endangered species. About 50 years ago, only 15 whooping cranes were alive. This species began to die out when people moved into the areas where the birds lived. Another problem for the whooping crane is that they lay only two eggs in a year. Nearly always, one of the new little birds dies.

With help from humans, whooping cranes might not become extinct. More than 140 birds are now alive. Scientists are using many methods that help newly hatched and adult birds survive. The governments of both Canada and the United States have laws that make it a crime to shoot the birds or harm them in other ways. The places where they breed and where they spend winters are protected wildlife areas. Even with these efforts, though, the number of living whooping cranes is so small that it may not be possible to keep the species from becoming extinct.

An endangered species that has a better chance at survival than the whooping crane is the gray wolf. Gray wolves used to live throughout the Northern Hemisphere.

◀ Although its environment seems harsh, this kind of cypress tree isn't endangered. It's not always obvious why a species becomes endangered.

The gray wolf became endangered partly because people moved into places where the wolves used to live. People made changes that made it harder for animals and plants to survive in their environment. An even bigger problem for wolves, though, is that people shoot them and poison them. Many people think that wolves are dangerous, although wolves don't attack humans. Ranchers try to get rid of wolves because they sometimes kill livestock. In most parts of the United States, it's now against the law to kill or harm the gray wolf.

- What kinds of environmental changes might affect the birth rate of a species? What activities or changes might affect the death rate?

- What could cause plant species to become extinct?

- Why do you think the gray wolf may have a better chance of surviving than the whooping crane?

▲ The horned guan lives in mountain forests. Its survival is endangered by the clearing of forests.

▼ A gray wolf

Think!

When a species becomes extinct, how are other species affected?

Identify Problems: Is It Living?

Think Tank Road Map

Just what makes something a living thing? Scientists have been asking this question for many years. You might think this would be a simple question to answer, but it's often quite difficult. Sea coral, for instance, can look like colorful rock, but it's actually a living animal. Scientists continue to discover new facts about living and nonliving things. How do they decide which is which?

15 • In Lesson 15 you'll identify the problems you'll face in deciding whether something is living or nonliving.

16 • In Lesson 16 you'll find some possible solutions to those problems.

17 • In Lesson 17 you'll choose a model for presenting your exhibits of living and nonliving things.

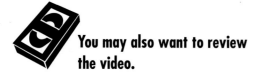 You may also want to review the video.

Problem: Your team of biologists is going to open a museum. The exhibits will show both living and nonliving things and explain how easy it is to confuse them. To build a good exhibit, you'll have to decide what makes something a living thing.

↓ Make a list of the problems you might face in choosing living and nonliving things for your museum. The questions below will help you.

1 What have you already learned about life processes that could help you decide whether something is living or nonliving?

2 What are some differences between living and nonliving things? (Review the list of living things you made in the Exploration in Lesson 2.)

3 What do you need to know about an object to decide whether it is living or not? How would it help to examine the parts of the object?

4 The pictures on the right show some organisms that puzzled scientists who study life processes. How did scientists decide whether these things were living or nonliving? What clues did they look for?

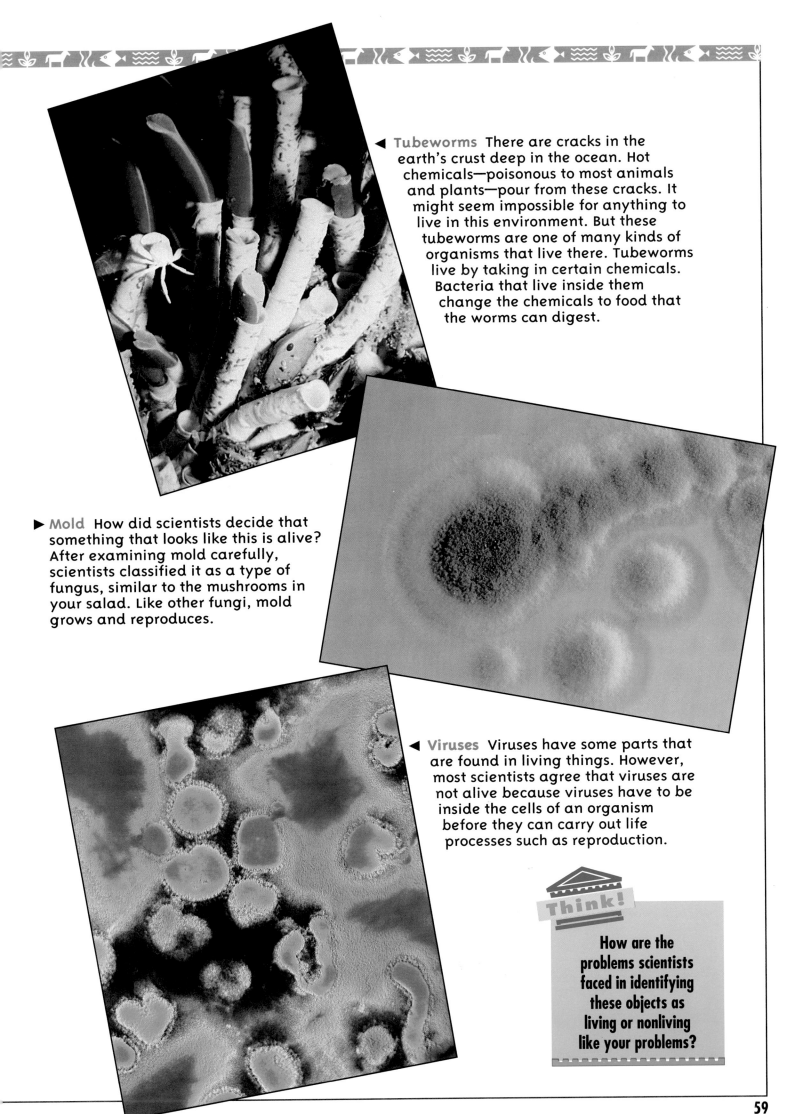

Tubeworms There are cracks in the earth's crust deep in the ocean. Hot chemicals—poisonous to most animals and plants—pour from these cracks. It might seem impossible for anything to live in this environment. But these tubeworms are one of many kinds of organisms that live there. Tubeworms live by taking in certain chemicals. Bacteria that live inside them change the chemicals to food that the worms can digest.

▶ **Mold** How did scientists decide that something that looks like this is alive? After examining mold carefully, scientists classified it as a type of fungus, similar to the mushrooms in your salad. Like other fungi, mold grows and reproduces.

◀ **Viruses** Viruses have some parts that are found in living things. However, most scientists agree that viruses are not alive because viruses have to be inside the cells of an organism before they can carry out life processes such as reproduction.

Think!

How are the problems scientists faced in identifying these objects as living or nonliving like your problems?

Find Solutions: Is It Living?

So you want to be a biologist.

People working in the field of biology do explorations and gather data just as you did in this unit. Because there are many kinds of living things, there are different kinds of biologists.

Botanists study plants, their parts, how they grow, and how they make food. Zoologists study the parts and behavior of animals. Microbiologists study living things that are so small they can be seen only with a microscope. These are just three areas of biology, and there are many more. But no matter what areas biologists specialize in, they all study the parts and processes of living things.

You've just identified some problems scientists faced in identifying living things. Now you'll take a closer look at mold. Studying the steps other scientists took when they identified mold might help you and your team decide why the things you put in your museum are classified as living or nonliving.

1

Look at the problems you listed in the last lesson. Beside each problem, try to list a similar problem facing the scientists who studied mold. You might not always be able to think of a matching problem.

2

Study the photographs of mold. What life processes did scientists observe that helped them decide whether mold was living? How might these observations help you explain the things in your exhibit?

3

On your list of problems facing the scientists who studied mold, record the solutions they came up with.

4

On your list of problems for your museum, record any solutions you can think of. Use both words and pictures.

Mold reproducing Molds grow from tiny powderlike objects called spores. These spores float through the air like the seeds of a dandelion. When the spores land on certain living or once-living things, they begin to grow. Mature molds make new spores that begin their own journey through the air.

Mold feeding Molds can't catch their food as animals do or make their food as plants do. Molds don't have chlorophyll—the green matter plants use to make food. Instead, molds absorb food materials from other living things or rotting matter. Some molds even live on other fungi.

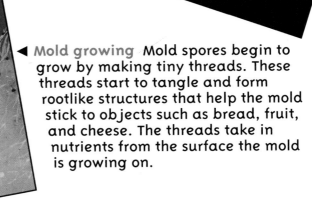

Mold growing Mold spores begin to grow by making tiny threads. These threads start to tangle and form rootlike structures that help the mold stick to objects such as bread, fruit, and cheese. The threads take in nutrients from the surface the mold is growing on.

Other resources you can check:

- To find out more about mold: *The Science Book of Things That Grow,* by Neil Ardley. Gulliver, 1991.

- To find out more about microscopic life forms: *The Smallest Life Around Us,* by Lucia Anderson. Crown Publishers, 1987.

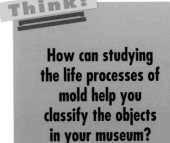

Think!

How can studying the life processes of mold help you classify the objects in your museum?

Make Models: Is It Living?

You and your team have identified problems you'll face in deciding whether things are living or nonliving. You've also found possible solutions to those problems. Now you can use those solutions to make decisions about the exhibits in your museum.

Possible models for presenting your opinion:

Debate If teams chose the same objects but made different decisions about what was living and what was nonliving, have a debate.

Diagram Draw a diagram of your exhibit, labeling each object and explaining why it is living or nonliving.

3-Dimensional Model Use real objects to build the exhibits in your museum. Include labels and captions.

Written Description Write a guide book for your museum, describing your exhibits and how you made your choices.

Oral Presentation Give a guided tour of your museum to visitors.

1

Bring to school some objects that you want to include in your museum. With your team, carefully study them.

2

Write a list of questions you can ask about every object to decide whether or not it is living. Make "yes" and "no" columns. As you examine each object, discuss it with other members of your team. Mark the correct column on your chart.

3

Decide whether each object is living or nonliving. Decide whether there is anything else you want to include in your exhibit.

4

Choose a model for presenting your exhibits. Be convincing! Use what you've learned about living and nonliving things to make your point.

5

Look at all the models your class has made. How did other teams decide what was living and what was nonliving?

6

How would your models have been different if you hadn't learned about life processes in this unit? What were the most important things you learned that helped you classify objects as living or nonliving?

Resources for classifying your objects:

• Your journals or LabMats from the Explorations in the unit contain valuable data.

• Look at the information in Lessons 1–14 of this unit.

• The reference books you've used in this unit are filled with information about the life processes of living things.

• Refer to the Video Clue Log. What life processes did the Science Sleuths investigate? How might you consider these processes when classifying your objects?

• If you're having problems, offer to trade information with another team.

Think!

How did making models of your exhibits help you think of problems and solutions you missed before?

FOR SCIENCE BROWSERS

© Franklin Jay Viola/Comstock Inc.

All articles reprinted with permission.

Simply Sponges

by Jerry Dunn
from *National Geographic World*

Living the Simple Life

WELL, DUH-H-H! A sponge doesn't have a brain in its head. Actually, it doesn't even have a head—or eyes, ears, mouth, heart, lungs, backbone, or legs.

It's no wonder people used to think sponges were plants. These squishy dwellers of the deep stay attached to one spot for their whole lives, just sitting there like vegetables. "Cuttings" snipped off grow into new sponges. But scientists observed that sponges eat food instead of manufacturing their own nourishment, as most plants do. It was elementary: Sponges were simple animals.

Brain or no brain, sponges have been surviving in Earth's waters for more than 500 million years. Scientists classify the 5,000 different species by their skeletons. The skeletons may be of limestone or glasslike needles or, sometimes, of a fibrous material called spongin.

Natural sponges with spongin skeletons soak up more water than synthetic ones. But today synthetic sponges are used almost exclusively for most household chores. It's less costly to manufacture them than to harvest live ones. Harvesters are usually divers who cut the sponges off and bring them up to be dried and cleaned. Their fate? To make your bath a more naturally absorbing experience! —*May 1993*

TOTALLY TUBULAR! These yellow tube sponges grow in the West Indies.

Why Do Leaves Change Color in the Fall?

by Nina Bassuk
from *SuperScience Blue*

Here's what botanist (plant scientist) Nina Bassuk says:

Every fall, the leaves of some trees turn yellow, orange, red, and purple. To understand why, try this:

Drop pieces of tree leaves in a dish of rubbing alcohol. Cover the dish with plastic wrap. After a few hours, what color are the leaf pieces? The alcohol? Let the pieces soak overnight, then look again.

The green color that leaked out of the leaves is a chemical called *chlorophyll* (KLOR-uh-fil). Without chlorophyll in its leaves, a tree would starve. That's because a leaf's job is to make tree food—a kind of sugar. The tree collects the ingredients it needs: sunlight, water, and carbon dioxide gas. But it's the chlorophyll in the leaf that starts changing the ingredients into sugar.

Leaves need plenty of sunlight, moisture, and warmth to make food. So when do they churn out the most of it? In summer!

With fall come shorter days, plus cooler and drier weather. So in many places, leaves stop making food. The chlorophyll inside breaks down into other, colorless chemicals.

That makes the green disappear from the leaves. But where do all the reds and golds come from? Some colors, like yellow and orange, were in the leaves all the time. They were just hidden by the green chlorophyll. (Did you see these colors in your experiment?)

Other colors, like red and purple, are made by a chemical reaction when sunlight hits the leaf. So if this fall is sunny, look for lots of red! —*October 1993* ◆

Slippery Seeds

Have you ever tried to pick up a wet watermelon seed? You get it between your thumb and forefinger and— *zooooom!* Off it goes. The witch-hazel plant does that to its own slippery, pointed seeds. After a witch-hazel pod opens, it pinches the seed. That pinch makes the seed shoot as far as 10 m (33 ft) to a place where it can sprout and grow without competition from its parent plant.

"want a lift?"

Shells For Homes

A hermit crab usually lives in an abandoned seashell that it carries from place to place. The seashell protects the hermit crab's soft body. Sometimes, a hermit crab adds an extra bit of protection to its borrowed home: The crab will attach a small sea anemone, an animal with poisonous stinging cells, to its sea shell. A larger animal that might otherwise try to eat the crab will leave it alone to avoid being stung by the anemone.

How Animals Survive Winter in Yellowstone

by James Halfpenny
excerpt from *Ranger Rick*

Winter is a great time for a scientist like me to spy on wild animals. And my favorite place to check them out is Yellowstone National Park. Snow turns the park into a wonderland. And everything is so peaceful in winter. That's because most visitors stay away when the snow gets deep.

I'm always amazed at how well some animals survive in weather that's 40° below zero. And I'm not talking about the *hibernators* (HI-bur-nay-turs)—the ones that sleep the winter away deep inside their burrows. Lots of other animals, such as the moose, survive in weather so cold you could hardly stand it. How do they do it?

A Thick, White Blanket

One way to survive is to use the snow as a blanket. When mice dig tunnels under the snow, the snow keeps their body heat from escaping into the cold outside air. The snow also keeps the bitter-cold wind away from them. So the mice are *much* warmer inside their snow tunnels than they would be outside. The blanket of snow also helps the mice hide from their enemies.

Mice live beneath the snow all winter long. They build their tunnels along the surface of the ground

Nibble, nibble, little elk (right). *Under the snow there's a bit of dry grass. That's about the best food an elk can find in winter.*

(see drawing below). They use the tunnels to get from one place to another and to find food.

Once in a while, a mouse comes to the surface of the snow. It may need a breath of fresh air. And it may want to check to see whether spring has come. Or, if its tunnel runs into a hard ice wall, the mouse may come up to look for softer snow. Then it will start digging a new tunnel.

Mice usually wait till it's dark out before they leave their tunnels. That way their enemies are less likely to catch them. But a dark mouse on white snow is still pretty easy for owls and coyotes to see, even at night. So watch out, mice!

snow

tunnel—

ground

© Frank Fretz

Diving Into Tunnels

Even *under* the snow, mice aren't safe from enemies—especially when the snow is shallow and soft. Coyotes hunt for them by listening for tiny squeaks. When a coyote hears a squeak, it springs high into the air. Then it dives nose-first through the soft snow. Sometimes the coyote comes up with a mouse in its mouth. Often it misses, though. And if the snow is deep or the surface is icy, the coyote may go hungry.

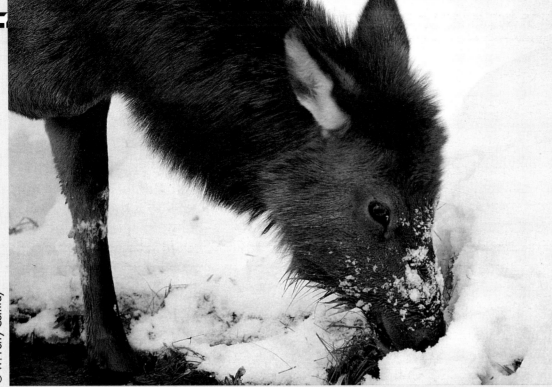

© W. Perry Conway

Snow Sinkers

Large animals are too big to run around in tunnels under the snow. So they have to do the best they can on the surface. Trouble is, many animals sink into the snow, which really slows them down. And animals that can't move fast often become easy prey. So how do big animals survive when deep snow is everywhere?

Moose can pull their long legs out of chest-deep snow as they walk. And they can stand on their hind legs to nibble high branches. But elk, deer, and bison have to struggle as much as we do when *we* try to walk through deep snow. And the snow makes finding food even harder for these animals. The grass they like to eat may be buried under deep snow.

Feet Made for Snow

It's much easier to walk on top of the snow than through it. And having big feet helps keep an animal from sinking in. Take snowshoe hares, for example. Their huge, furry feet help them travel fast on the surface to escape predators.

But—too bad for the hares in Yellowstone—one of their predators *also* has big feet. A lynx can travel on top of the snow just as well as a hare can. Both of them just skim across the surface.

Yellowstone is unlike any other place on Earth. That's why it's such a great place to study animals in winter. —*December 1993* ◆

Fluffy, furry feet help the lynx and the snowshoe hare skim across the top of the snow.

© Leonard Lee Rue III

Seahorse Fathers

Male seahorses are very responsible fathers. The female lays her eggs in a pouch on the male's belly. He cares for the eggs by himself until they hatch.

Air-Cleaning Plants

Plants in your home or classroom can actually clean the air you breathe. Plants remove many dangerous gases from the air. The leaves take in the gases. Then the gases move through the plant down to its roots, where microscopic organisms eat the gases! Corn plants and chrysanthemums will clean the air in a room during the day; jade plants and cacti will clean the air at night.

Head South—But Which Way Is That?

by Jack Myers

excerpt from *Highlights*

Most animals don't do as much thinking as people do. Instead, they use instincts—built-in programs that tell them what to do. Scientists call instincts programmed behavior.

A good example of programmed behavior is bird migration. Young birds don't need to be taught how to migrate—they just do it. They get ready by growing new feathers and storing fat to give energy for the long journey. Then, at the right time of the year, they fly off in the right direction, heading south for warmer weather.

Scientists have been especially curious about one part of that migration program: How do birds tell which way is south? It didn't take many experiments to find that birds have a magnetic sense. They must have some kind of built-in compass, though we don't know exactly how it works. But there's more to the problem.

A compass is great for finding your way in case you get lost in the woods. But it isn't perfect. It points to the earth's magnetic pole, which is in northern Canada and about one thousand miles from the North Pole you'd see on a map. So if you're a sailor on a long ocean voyage you can't trust your compass needle. You have to correct it.

Two scientists have found out how one bird corrects its [internal] compass. They studied the Savannah sparrow, a bird that migrates at night. They brought up young sparrows in the laboratory where they were not able to see older birds or the outside world.

When the birds were about a month old they were divided into four groups and put in four different cages. The cages were put in a round room, with each in a different location. The room's ceiling was an artificial sky made of a plastic disk with sixteen light spots for "stars." The sky was slowly rotated to turn one time around every twenty-four hours. The birds were kept in their cages each night for almost a month.

In September, when the birds were ready to migrate, they were taken one by one to another round, dimly lit room. The test was to see

which way they would start hopping. Every bird knew which way it wanted to go.

But though all four groups had their magnetic compasses working all right, each group thought that south was in a different direction. The four groups corrected their compasses in four different ways. They had done that by watching the artificial night sky from different directions.

When you need to find your direction at night you look for the North Star. Other stars slowly move around the sky at night. But the North Star doesn't seem to move at all. It happens to be at a special place in the sky. Wherever you are it lines up with the earth's North Pole.

You have to look hard to find the North Star. First you find the Big Dipper and its two pointer stars. They point toward the North Star in the handle of the Little Dipper.

Birds don't do all that. If we could read their built-in program it would say: "Find the one place in the night sky that never moves. Correct your compass so that it points to that place. Then fly in the opposite direction. That's where you want to go." —*September 1993* ◆

Changing Groupers
Groupers are fish that live on or near coral reefs. Every grouper starts its life as a female and can lay many eggs. If a grouper survives to a certain age, it changes to a male!

Excerpt from *Our National Parks*
by John Muir

...**O**f all the birds of the high Sierra, the strangest, noisiest, and most notable is the Clarke crow. He is a foot long, ashy gray in color, with black wings, white tail, and a strong, sharp bill, with which he digs into the pine cones for seeds.

He is quick, jerky, and irregular in his movements and speech, and makes a loud and showy advertisement of himself—swooping and diving in deep curves across gorges and valleys from ridge to ridge. He flies like a woodpecker, hammers dead limbs for insects, digs big holes in pine cones to get at the seeds, cracks nuts held between his toes, cries like a crow or jay—but in a far louder, harsher, and more forbidding tone of voice—and besides his crow caws and screams, has a great variety of small chatter talk.

Once when I made my camp in a grove at Cathedral Lake, I chanced to leave a cake of soap on the shore where I had been washing, and a few minutes afterward I saw my soap flying past me through the grove, pushed by a Clarke crow.

Even in winter, in calm weather, he stays in his high mountain home, defying the bitter frost. Once I lay snowbound through a three days' storm at the timber-line on Mount Shasta; and while the roaring snow-laden blast swept by, one of these brave birds came to my camp, and began hammering at the cones on the topmost branches of half-buried pines. —*January 1902* ◆

GLOSSARY

Concept vocabulary and other technical terms

anther [an'·thər]: *n.* The flower part that produces pollen; it is the top part of the stamen.

carbon dioxide [kär'·bən dī·ox'·sīd]: *n.* A gas present in air; it is used by plants to make food and is formed as a waste as cells obtain energy from food.

carnivore [kär'·nə·vôr]: *n.* An animal that eats mainly meat.

cell [sel]: *n.* The smallest living unit of an organism; every living thing is made up of one or more cells.

endangered species [in·dān'·jərd spē'·shēz]: *n.* A species of organism that is in danger of becoming extinct because so few of its kind are alive.

food chain [fōod chān]: *n.* Organisms that are connected by the food they eat; a simple food chain often begins with a plant, which makes its own food, and continues with an organism that feeds on the plant, followed by an organism that feeds on the plant-eating organism.

herbivore [hûr'·bə·vôr]: *n.* An animal that eats mainly plants.

life cycle [līf sī'·kəl]: *n.* The unending series of changes that occurs as an organism develops from an egg to an adult, which then reproduces and so continues the cycle.

life processes [līf pros'·es·ez]: *n.* The activities needed to keep living things alive and species in existence.

metamorphosis [met·ə·môr'·fə·sis]: *n.* The set of changes some organisms go through as they develop from egg to adult.

omnivore [om'·ni·vôr]: *n.* An animal that eats both plants and meat.

organ [ôr'·gən]: *n.* A group of different kinds of tissues that work together; the heart is an organ.

organism [ôr'·gə·niz·əm]: *n.* A living thing.

ovary [ōv'·ə·rē]: *n.* Part of the pistil of a flower; the ovary produces eggs and develops into a fruit.

oxygen [ok'·si·jən]: *n.* A gas present in air; most organisms use oxygen as their cells get energy from food.

photosynthesis [fōt·ō·sin'·thə·sis]: *n.* The process by which plants and some other organisms make their own food; the organisms use light energy to put together water and carbon dioxide, forming glucose, a sugar.

pistil [pis'·təl]: *n.* The flower part that catches pollen and produces eggs.

species [spē'·shēz]: *n.* A kind of living thing; a lion, a tiger, and a house cat are three different species of cat.

stamen [stā'·mən]: *n.* The flower part that produces pollen in the structure called the anther.

system [sis'·təm]: *n.* Different kinds of organs that work together; some examples are the digestive system, the respiratory system, and the skeletal system.

tissue [tish'·ōō]: *n.* A group of cells, all of the same kind, that work together; nerve tissue is an example.

a	add, map	ī	ice, write	û(r)	burn, term
ā	ace, rate	o	odd, hot	yōō	fuse, few
â(r)	care, air	ō	open, so	ə	a in above
ä	palm, father	ô	order, jaw		e in sicken
e	end, pet	ŏŏ	took, full		i in possible
ē	equal, tree	ōō	pool, food		o in melon
i	it, give	u	up, done		u in circus

INDEX

Page references in *italics* indicate illustrations, photographs, and tables.